Cambridge Elements

Elements in the Philosophy of Ludwig Wittgenstein
edited by
David G. Stern
University of Iowa

STYLE, METHOD AND PHILOSOPHY IN WITTGENSTEIN

Alois Pichler
University of Bergen

Shaftesbury Road, Cambridge CB2 8EA, United Kingdom

One Liberty Plaza, 20th Floor, New York, NY 10006, USA

477 Williamstown Road, Port Melbourne, VIC 3207, Australia

314–321, 3rd Floor, Plot 3, Splendor Forum, Jasola District Centre, New Delhi – 110025, India

103 Penang Road, #05–06/07, Visioncrest Commercial, Singapore 238467

Cambridge University Press is part of Cambridge University Press & Assessment, a department of the University of Cambridge.

We share the University's mission to contribute to society through the pursuit of education, learning and research at the highest international levels of excellence.

www.cambridge.org
Information on this title: www.cambridge.org/9781009462792
DOI: 10.1017/9781108955485

© Alois Pichler 2023

This publication is in copyright. Subject to statutory exception and to the provisions of relevant collective licensing agreements, no reproduction of any part may take place without the written permission of Cambridge University Press & Assessment.

First published 2023

A catalogue record for this publication is available from the British Library

ISBN 978-1-009-46279-2 Hardback
ISBN 978-1-108-95807-3 Paperback
ISSN 2632-7112 (online)
ISSN 2632-7104 (print)

Cambridge University Press & Assessment has no responsibility for the persistence or accuracy of URLs for external or third-party internet websites referred to in this publication and does not guarantee that any content on such websites is, or will remain, accurate or appropriate.

Style, Method and Philosophy in Wittgenstein

Elements in the Philosophy of Ludwig Wittgenstein

DOI: 10.1017/9781108955485
First published online: September 2023

Alois Pichler
University of Bergen

Author for correspondence: Alois Pichler, alois.pichler@uib.no

Abstract: Wittgenstein said, 'really one should write philosophy only as one writes a poem'. This Element provides a comprehensive explanation of what he possibly meant by the statement, and why the statement is a correct description of Wittgenstein's philosophy. It connects the statement with Wittgenstein's idea of philosophical clarification, the methods he uses in it and the masters he acknowledges as the sources for his ways of 'moving his thought'. The Element introduces distinctions that are essential for approaching the multilayered complex of Wittgenstein's oeuvre. One is the distinction between writing philosophical clarifications for himself on the one hand and forming philosophical books for his reader on the other. While poetry was central to both activities, it was mandatory for the second. Indeed, for creating the perfect philosophical book, Wittgenstein thought he lacked precisely what some of his masters possessed: poetic genius.

Keywords: style, method, poetry, writing, philosophical work

© Alois Pichler 2023

ISBNs: 9781009462792 (HB), 9781108958073 (PB), 9781108955485 (OC)
ISSNs: 2632-7112 (online), 2632-7104 (print)

Contents

Introduction 1

1 Writing Philosophy; Forming Philosophical Works 6

2 Methods for the Apt Movement of Thought 23

3 Poetry in Philosophy 41

References 66

Style, Method and Philosophy in Wittgenstein 1

Introduction

It is not uncommon to draw attention to or even admire Wittgenstein's *Tractatus Logico-Philosophicus* or his *Philosophical Investigations* for their literary style. But the relation between the style and form of the books and their philosophy is a matter of dispute. Some claim that the two sides are intimately related and draw attention to the form of Wittgenstein's writings as a prerequisite for understanding his philosophy.[1] 'Resolute' readers consider frame content,[2] whereas other readers consider tree-structured readings imperative for interpreting the *Tractatus*.[3] For yet others, the form of Wittgenstein's works is sufficiently accidental to his arguments and methods such that one can disregard it. Wittgenstein's style can even be considered an idiosyncratic deficit that hinders and obscures understanding Wittgenstein the philosopher.[4] Some argue that Wittgenstein himself deemed the album form of the *Investigations* a serious shortcoming caused by an alleged incapability to produce a linear and systematic text.[5] Glock contrasts the *Investigations* album with the *Blue Book*, which 'is neither aphoristic (as the *Tractatus* and *Philosophical Investigations*) nor truncated (as his lecture notes) but discursive'.[6] While Anscombe agreed that Wittgenstein's *Blue Book* 'is more like a regular piece of philosophic writing than ... anything of any length that he wrote in the last twenty years of his life', she early opposed the personal shortcoming view: 'There was never any question of his writing the *Investigations* except in the form of just such discrete chunks as we have there.'[7]

This Element develops the discussion further by offering the following threefold approach: (1) looking at the respective *forms* of the philosophical works that Wittgenstein prepared for his readers; (2) attending to the *methods* that Wittgenstein uses for the forming of those works as well as for his overall work of clarification ('Klärungswerk'; CV 19/16);[8] and (3) trying to understand Wittgenstein's statement that 'really one should write philosophy only as one *writes a poem*' ('Philosophie dürfte man eigentlich nur *dichten*'; CV 24/28). It is reasonable to expect that an intimate relation between Wittgenstein's style and his philosophy will reveal itself in Wittgenstein's forming of his philosophical works. The specific form of each of these will then tell us something important about his philosophy at the time. Furthermore, style and form will then also be

---

[1] For example, Cavell 2004; Pichler 2004 and Erbacher 2015.
[2] For example, Diamond 1991: 19 and Conant 1997.   [3] For example, Bazzocchi 2014.
[4] For example, Glock 2004 and Kanterian 2012.   [5] For example, Hilmy 1987: 15–17.
[6] Glock 1996: 23.
[7] Anscombe 1969: 374. For brief outlines of the discussion, see Kahane et al. 2007: 19–25 and Stern 2017: 41–4.
[8] Reference to CV is as follows: the page numbers before the slash refer to the 1980 edition, the page numbers after the slash to the 1998 edition.

integral parts of Wittgenstein's methods for moving his thoughts and texts productively forward – he calls them 'Gedankenbewegungen' (CV 19/16).

I argue that Wittgenstein's work of clarification proceeds on two levels: one is the activity of philosophical clarification for himself through writing, lecturing and discussion; the other is the activity of composing works for the reader so that they can clarify their own philosophical concepts and problems. The first is the level of Wittgenstein's own, authentic philosophical reactions; the second is the level of additionally forming out of the 'precipitate'[9] from these reactions a conducive book for the reader. Naturally, the two are not entirely separated and can also go hand in hand. A related and widely accepted distinction is the one between non-works and works among Wittgenstein's writings.[10] Von Wright, for example, distinguishes between Wittgenstein's 'philosophical works' and his 'philosophical texts' (CV Preface/ix) and speaks of 'the various "layers of composition" of works' (1982: 60). The distinction and relation between the two levels will be foremostly treated in Section 1 but it informs the entire Element.

In a remark from the spring of 1932, Wittgenstein acknowledges that he has received his methods and ways of moving his thought – his 'Gedankenbewegungen' – from others, and then he lists ten figures. The ten are central to Section 2. This section also includes a study of Wittgenstein's use of the word 'Gedankenbewegung'. It is a difficult word to translate. Literally, it means 'movement of thought(s)'. In Wittgenstein, the word designates ways of moving thoughts forward in a way that is conducive to the work of clarification, again on both of its levels. It thus includes methods and strategies for efficiently proceeding from one thought to the other. I will, in addition to 'move', 'movement of thought' or 'train of thought', use 'method' and 'strategy' as translations. One can expect that if there is a unity of style and philosophy in Wittgenstein, then it will again come to the fore in the methods he chose for forming his philosophical works or books for the reader. One of the ten figures, Frege, will turn out to be seminal for the forming of at least two of Wittgenstein's philosophical works, the *Tractatus* and the *Brown Book*. So will two others among the ten, Spengler and Schopenhauer: the former for the *Brown Book* and the latter for the *Investigations*.

Finally, the strength and nature of an intimate connection between Wittgenstein's philosophy and style should also become manifest through an examination of Wittgenstein's own, above cited, statement about the strong link between philosophy and 'Dichtung'/'dichten'. This examination is carried out in Section 3. Also the German word 'dichten' is difficult to translate. Rather

---

[9] I am indebted to Jérôme Letourneur for making me think more about Wittgenstein using the expression 'precipitate' ('Niederschlag'). See also Erbacher 2015: 20 and Uffelmann 2018: 189.
[10] See Keicher 2000; Pichler 2009; Rothhaupt 2010; Erbacher 2015; Stern 2017 and, naturally, von Wright 1982.

than only poetry and poems, 'Dichtung' means any form of creative writing, including narrative, lyric and drama. It thus goes beyond what is meant by the English expressions 'fiction' and 'imaginative literature'. Together with 'Erdichtung', it is often used in the sense of confabulation. For lack of a better translation, I'll use 'poetry', 'poet' ('Dichter') and 'poetic' ('dichterisch'), although these words suggest too much of an affinity with poems.[11]

Schalkwyk translates 'dichten' as 'poetize' and connects the statement with Wittgenstein's lasting 'concept of the inexpressible' and his 'turning away, in his later work, from the search for an unsituated – we might say "philosophical" – perspective, to the insight that language can be defined only in terms of its situation'. Moreover, he stresses Wittgenstein's employment of fiction as grammatical investigation. Also Janik argues that Wittgenstein's philosophy invites imaginative fiction; it conducts philosophical clarification by 'creating fictive natural histories that illuminate our actual one' and becomes in parts 'philosophische Dichtung'/'gedichtete Philosophie'. Venturinha similarly argues that Wittgenstein appreciates poetry for its imaginative capacity to offer 'views from nowhere', forcing us to abandon our 'presuppositions about the common meanings of words and to instinctively reflect upon new relations of concepts, be they possible or not'. Perloff sees the link in the fact that philosophy, 'as Wittgenstein sees it, is a form of continual reinvention with a view to making language more functional, the ideal being the precision of numbers'. She connects the statement with Wittgenstein's remark that there is a 'queer resemblance between a philosophical investigation (perhaps especially in mathematics) and one in aesthetics' (CV 25/29).[12] My conclusion is that Wittgenstein's statement needs to be connected with the role that he assigns to the genius for philosophy which again brings us back to Schopenhauer, Weininger and Spengler – three of the ten figures Wittgenstein acknowledges as sources for methods that he uses in his work of clarification. Wittgenstein regarded using poetry as integral to both the activity of philosophical clarification for himself and the activity of forming philosophical books for the reader. But he gravely felt that he did not live up to the ideal he set himself regarding the form his philosophical work should take. At the same time, he believed that a poetic genius could achieve the ideal.

Wittgenstein contends that philosophical problems are problems of conceptual confusion that require conceptual rather than factual investigations (§383, RPP I §949, Z §458). Philosophical problems arise from wrong conceptions and concepts, and are solved or dissolved (BBB 47) by showing that they are based on wrong concepts and in fact are without substance, superfluous, purely

---

[11] For a general discussion of issues in translating 'Dichtung', see Décultot 2014.
[12] Schalkwyk 2004: 55–7, 66; Janik 2006: 158; Janik 2018: 151; Venturinha 2018: 166; Perloff 2004: 42.

'ornamental'. The confusions can arise when 'language is, as it were, idling, not when it is doing work' (§132) – for example when a word is misused, or the grammar of a word misunderstood. In the *Blue Book* Wittgenstein calls this a 'grammatical misunderstanding' (BBB 8), in the *Tractatus* he had spoken of 'misunderstanding the logic of language'. In *Nachlass* Ms-110,184 (20.6.1931) Wittgenstein acknowledges Ernst (1910) as his source for this wording.[13] One of the methods proposed by Wittgenstein for finding a way out of the philosophical problem is to clarify the philosophical use of the word by bringing it back ('zurückführen', §116) to the place where it does its work. For the early Wittgenstein, this place was logic as it presents itself in language analysed. For the later Wittgenstein, the concepts that philosophy is concerned with are at work in everyday language. Consequently, much of the later Wittgenstein, but not necessarily the Wittgenstein of the *Investigations*, will want to bring philosophy back to language as used in everyday life and acting, that is the 'language-game' (§7). 'Zurückführen' is yet another word that is difficult to translate. The word is used by Wittgenstein, Frege, Weininger, Schopenhauer and many others in a great number of different contexts. Translating it into English with just one expression is impossible. 'Reduce' suggests reductionism, but I will use it as the translation in a few places where the reductionist aspect is included. In the context of Wittgenstein's use of the term, I will use 'return', 'bring (back)' or even 'bring home' as Wittgenstein himself speaks of 'the language in which [a word] is at home' ('Heimat'; §116). In the context of Frege's use, I will predominantly use 'transform'. Occasionally I shall, as a reminder, also put the German word in parentheses next to the translation.

Three methods that play a vital role on both levels of Wittgenstein's work of clarification are using language-games for bringing words and concepts of philosophy back ('zurückführen') to where they are doing work; producing perspicuous representations ('übersichtliche Darstellung'; §122)[14] of the depth grammar of language so that the philosopher sees the connections required for dealing with their problems; and using analogies, pictures and the poetic ('Dichtung') more generally for moving philosophical thought productively forward ('Gedankenbewegung'). I will exemplify how style and philosophy

---

[13] For an introduction to Wittgenstein's *Nachlass* and its different 'strata', see von Wright 1982: 39–43. All reference to *Nachlass* items is by Ms-/Ts-, followed by the number of the item given in von Wright's catalogue (von Wright 1969; revised in von Wright 1982 and later editions) and the BNE; 'Ms-110,184', for example, refers to page 184 in Wittgenstein *Nachlass* manuscript 110. Citations from the *Nachlass* follow the BNE; translations of *Nachlass* passages are, unless indicated otherwise, mine. For passages that are in print, a citation to the published title is provided; if not indicated otherwise, all references marked by '§' and 'Preface' refer to the *Philosophical Investigations*.
[14] 'Übersichtliche Darstellung' is yet another expression difficult to translate; for a brief discussion, see Baker and Hacker 2005a: 307–8.

are intertwined in Wittgenstein's works with particular attention to the method of perspicuous representation.

I argue that seeing the *Investigations* in the right light involves contrasting it not only with the *Tractatus* but also with the *Brown Book*, and that the contrast is most visible in the different styles, forms and methods that each of the three works takes. In the early 1930s, Wittgenstein optimistically thought that when the real use of the word is unmasked and the philosopher is willing to let go of the problematic concept, the specific conceptual confusion and the problem can disappear *completely*. Already in the *Tractatus* we find that Wittgenstein believed that clarification can be *complete*, in fact, that *any* philosophical problem and concept can be *cleared away* by clearing away the *great* philosophical problem(s) and concepts. At a later point Wittgenstein still believed that one could at least clear away *completely* single, smaller size problems piecemeal ('Querstreifenphilosophie', BT 316). But the Wittgenstein of the *Investigations* doubts the possibility of attaining even this modest goal and claims to offer no more than a mirror in which the reader can recognise and understand their and others' specific philosophical problems as well as their sources and multiple entanglements. I argue that for each of these three different kinds of clarification project, questions of style and form are essential.

For the later Wittgenstein, philosophical clarification includes giving a perspicuous representation, an overview of the grammar of the word that is problematic for philosophy, as it functions in the context of everyday life and acting. Perspicuous representation in Wittgenstein can take very different forms, depending on, for example, whether complete clarification is thought possible even if only of partial problems and bit by bit, whether the goal becomes more one of self-understanding and self-insight, or whether the subject matter is the grammar of language rather than, for example, mathematics. In this Element, the focus is on perspicuous representation of the grammar of language. While the ultimate goal of a complete clearing away of philosophical conceptions and concepts might still have been on the horizon for the *Investigations*, the focus now was rather on assisting the reader in understanding themselves and the other as engaged in philosophy rather than as someone who is to leave philosophical concepts behind as quickly as possible. The *Investigations* preface states that the book can 'be seen in the right light only by contrast with and against the background of my old way of thinking'. Not surprisingly, in this Element the discussions of Wittgenstein's conception of philosophy will be intertwined with the discussions driven by the three main foci: the forming and forms of Wittgenstein's philosophical works; the ways of moving his philosophical thought and compositions productively forward that he adopted and adapted from others; and the intimate connection Wittgenstein establishes between philosophy and poetry.

1 Writing Philosophy; Forming Philosophical Works

1.1 *Nachlass* and Works

Philosophy is for Wittgenstein the activity of clarifying thought and language (TLP 4.112; §133). Wittgenstein could engage in this activity in conversation with a friend, in correspondence, in lecturing, in discussion with students and colleagues, in solitary thinking and in various other ways. But most of all he carried it out in writing. Philosophical writing also included drawing diagrams and figures,[15] doing calculations and proofs and occasionally also what just looks like scribbling.[16] It is his 20,000 page *Nachlass* that is the authentic witness of Wittgenstein's writing of philosophical clarifications.[17] The *Nachlass* contains the very 'reactions' that he experienced during clarification, while his books prepared for the reader are formed out of – as Wittgenstein himself says in the preface to the *Philosophical Investigations* – a 'precipitate' from those reactions. This means that for learning about and learning *from* Wittgenstein's own philosophical clarifications, we will have to attend also to the *Nachlass*, where his remarks 'perform their whole work' (MT 219; 6.3.1937), rather than only to the books Wittgenstein, or his editors, prepared for publication.[18] A second place to visit and to attend to are the detailed and minute records that we have of Wittgenstein's philosophical conversations, exchanges and lectures. In these sources we can see Wittgenstein at work in his conceptual investigations and follow his philosophical arguments as they develop authentically and get their work done. It should go without saying that the texts carrying his philosophical reaction are not Wittgenstein's last words on the matter. They should not be taken as offering settled philosophical statements. Rather than being the *outcome* of clarification, they often show the work of clarification as it is in progress, as it is actually being undertaken.

Next to his original philosophical reactions, the *Nachlass* contains also Wittgenstein's *works*, the books that he composed for the philosophical reader. What then are they? That the *Nachlass* – in addition to the sources for the *Tractatus* and the *Investigations* – contains still other, 'projected works'[19] was

---

[15] See Biggs 1998 and Nyíri 2006.
[16] For introductions to Wittgenstein's writing, see Pichler 2006 and Somavilla 2020. Many of Wittgenstein's analyses of his own writing are coded; Gorlée 2020 gives an analysis of the coded remarks from a semiotic point of view and offers many of them in English translation.
[17] For introductions to the *Nachlass*, see von Wright 1982, especially 'The Wittgenstein Papers', and Stern 1996.
[18] For a comprehensive assessment of the Wittgenstein trustees' work on editing Wittgenstein, see Wallgren 2023.
[19] McGuinness 2002b: 285.

already von Wright's view.[20] Schulte proposes three rules of thumb for establishing 'whether a certain manuscript or typescript is to count as a work by Wittgenstein': (1) Wittgenstein 'thought that the text in question formed a more or less organic whole displaying a satisfactory relation between form and content'; (2) 'we as readers can detect a line of argument with theses, supporting reasons, objections, examples, etc.'; and (3) 'the text has undergone a certain amount of stylistic polishing and rearranging of individual remarks showing that there has been some improvement in the direction of enhanced readability and intelligibility'.[21] Hence, the Wittgensteinian philosophical *work* is born out of careful selection, followed by labour-intensive collage, potentially several cycles of arrangement and rearrangement and, of course, detailed text revisions.[22] But, as a result, the work is often indeed much less discursive, less straightforward, less linear and less progressive in argumentation than the original sources from which it was composed.[23] The 'Philosophische Bemerkungen' of Ts-209 and the *Investigations* are good examples of the diminishing and fragmenting effect which Wittgenstein's methods for producing his works had on their linearity and discursiveness. Here we see that Schulte's criterion (2), emphasising the presence of a clear line of argument which is discernible by the reader, can mark as much the *non*-work as the work. For the work often manifests much less of a discursive and linear structure with formal argument than the non-work. Schulte himself states that criterion (2) is a criterion from the philosophical reader's perspective rather than from Wittgenstein's.[24]

The most important difference between the non-works and the works is that Wittgenstein seeks to give the works a form that is in full rapport with his philosophy at the time, such that there is 'a satisfactory relation between form and content'.[25] We can therefore assume that it is in the works that the connection between Wittgenstein's style and his philosophy becomes most visible and graspable. But before looking more into some of the specific forms his works received, we should try to better understand the challenges Wittgenstein found himself confronted with when wanting to compose out of his writing works, books for the reader.

---

[20] See for example von Wright 1982: 50.
[21] Schulte 2006: 402; other discussions include Stern 1996: 457–62, Pichler 2004: ch. 2.2, Moyal-Sharrock 2013: 355–61 and Stern 2017: 45–6. Pichler (2023) suggests additional indicators for distinguishing the works from the non-works.
[22] von Wright's studies of *Tractatus* and *Investigations* genesis (both included in von Wright 1982) as well as Krüger 1993 are early examples of studies of Wittgensteinian work composition.
[23] See also Stern 1996: 449.   [24] Schulte 2006: 404.   [25] Schulte 2006: 402.

1.2 Composing Philosophical Works

It was one thing for Wittgenstein to engage in philosophical activity by way of first writing, and a quite different thing to later transform what he had written into a book for the reader. Both required 'work with greatest care' (CV 34/39–40), but the second more so than the first. Philosophical clarification by first writing could consist in creating inner dialogues with and for himself, trying to get to grips with a tormenting philosophical problem by capturing it with the redeeming 'right expression' (§335). Sometimes, Wittgenstein finds that what he is best at is simply stating the philosophical problem at stake ('einfach ein Problem aussprechen', Ms-119,79v; 1937). Going further to compose from first writing – the very testimony of his philosophical clarifications and arguments, the 'record of the inner dialogue that was the driving force in the development of his philosophical work'[26] – a book for publication posed a different set of challenges. The reader might, for example, be unaware of or indifferent to the specific philosophical problem the clarification of which Wittgenstein wanted to share with them. Partly connected to this is also the challenge of coming up for the reader with the right kind of example.[27] Finally, there is the challenge of making the right selection of remarks. One thing is the redeeming word ('erlösende Wort'; BT 302) that comes to the philosopher as an expression permitting the philosopher to get hold of the 'hair on one's tongue' (BT 302), that is to finally put down in words the philosophical problem at hand. But it can be quite a different thing to reach the redeeming word that puts an end to the philosophical problem and actually enables us to dissolve it. If the reader doesn't have the specific problem to begin with, they won't experience the redeeming word as actually redeeming. The redeeming word, Wittgenstein says in 1944 (Ms-179,3v), functions like a capstone for a building. If the reader cannot follow Wittgenstein's development of a specific philosophical conception or problem, or cannot be awakened to it as a *problem*, they will not experience the redeeming word. 'What happens to work with me doesn't work with him (Prof. Moore) – works with me now, and may not work with me tomorrow' (WCL 196).

Of course, one should never expect a book to offer treatment and dissolution of *all* the philosophical problems that readers might have. But if it is possible to offer in *one* book a *complete* solution to *all* philosophical problems, then this would be the first thing to try out. This is what Wittgenstein aspired to when producing the *Tractatus Logico-Philosophicus*. Should that not be possible, then one should try to offer a piecemeal treatment of smaller size problems sufficiently representative and instructive for the reader to learn from and to go

---

[26] Stern 1996: 453.   [27] See also Perloff 2011: 724.

on with for the purpose of clarifying their *own* problems and concepts. This approach characterises much of the works of the so-called middle Wittgenstein, including the *Brown Book*. Should this also turn out to be either non-doable or maybe even inappropriate to the subject, the book could at least offer the following: a collection and arrangement of concepts and problems as well as attempts at clarification that help the reader in understanding themselves as a philosophical human being, whose concepts and problems can be variously misled and entangled with each other. This is what Wittgenstein tried to offer with the *Philosophical Investigations*, and as problems and attempts at clarification he shared a selection of his own as he had undertaken and experienced them since his return to Cambridge in 1929.

Trying to produce an apt offer of philosophy-by-piecemeal (e.g. in the *Brown Book*) and trying to produce (with the *Investigations*) an apt 'mirror' for the reader (CV 18/25), both turned out to be significantly more difficult than trying to do the alleged once-and-for-all solution that was attempted in the *Tractatus*. And each of the three methods for preparing a book for the reader was for Wittgenstein significantly more laborious than conducting philosophical clarification in first writing for himself. Offering his work with the *Investigations* in the form of an album and also *calling* it an album seemed eventually the right response. The *Investigations* album can be regarded as an invitation to not only read and learn from the book itself but to also go back to the places in the *Nachlass* where its remarks are fully available in their contexts of original reaction. But, ultimately, the remarks in the *Investigations* are only reminders of those original reactions, 'recollections' (§127).

To develop for the reader a fitting arrangement of his remarks was for Wittgenstein a painful torment. The apt movement or train of thought ('Gedankenbewegung') in the reader first required an apt movement and arrangement of Wittgenstein's own thought. The arrangement could not simply be the same arrangement that the remarks took in his own original clarifications. It was after all only a selection of the best parts of the original clarification activities that were to be shared with the reader. And it was only *examples* of them that were to be given. Composing out of his writings the right arrangement for the reader was a great challenge. It seems that Wittgenstein sought refuge in the idea of the power of the genius as it was described by Schopenhauer and others. A writer of character and genius rather than mere talent would be able to give their writing the right arrangement and suitable composition by simply following their *intuition* ('Anschauung').[28] Intuition is what characterises the genius and poet proper, they said. But Wittgenstein felt he could achieve his

---

[28] CV 35/40–1 *et passim* and Schopenhauer 1873: vol. II, ch. 31.

goal only through persistent hard work. The reason for this, he thought, was because in his own view he possessed only talent. While genius can be based on '*courage in one's talent*' (CV 38/44), he felt he lacked the required courage, and therefore did not think he was a genius (CV 18/16).[29] Still, since he at least had talent, he hoped he could develop the skills required for the forming of his philosophical books. He could also make good use of what he was able to pick up from others. As we will see, Wittgenstein gleaned methods for composition from the giants of writing and composition he had grown to admire.

1.3 The *Tractatus* Ladder of Philosophical Theses

It seems reasonable to regard the *Notes on Logic* from October 1913 as the earliest of all the philosophical works that are preserved in the *Nachlass*. Likewise, Ms-101, the first of the World War I diaries, can well be regarded as the earliest preserved document of first writing and genuine philosophical clarification in action. Ms-101 was begun in August 1914. Already by the autumn of 1915 (ICE: To Russell 22.10.1915), after writing several hundred pages of philosophical clarifications, Wittgenstein started anew on a summary of his philosophical activities signalling a new philosophical work. This became what later was published as *Prototractatus*. The summary consists of six sentences numbered 1 to 6.[30] For incorporating 'all the good sentences' from his 'other manuscripts' (Ms-104,III; 1916), Wittgenstein used the method of interpolation.[31] He did this by assigning to each of the sentences chosen from the manuscripts a decimal number (1.#, 2.# ...) and linking it to one of the first five chief sentences. The decimal numbering may continue several digits down (e.g. '4.100141'), thereby indicating the specific position allocated to the sentence *within* the entire group of sentences linked with the same chief sentence and giving the work 'perspicuity and clarity' (ICE: To von Ficker 5.12.1919). The thinking behind this method of composition foreshadows perspicuous representation and a remark from November 1930: there Wittgenstein says that his book is to be a work of *culture*. This implies that each and every one of the book's remarks is given its specific place where it can 'work in the spirit of the whole' (CV 8–9). The form of the book eventually emerging, the *Tractatus*, is the ladder (TLP 6.54; CV 7/10). With this ladder form, Wittgenstein thought he would be able to offer a solution to his and the reader's philosophical concepts and problems *once and for all* (TLP Preface).

The ladder of the *Tractatus* has seven rungs: its cardinal propositions 1–7. Originally it had only six rungs because initially the ladder was meant to end

---

[29] See CV 18–19/16, 35/40, 36/42 *et passim*. For a critical reflection and cultural-historical setting of Wittgenstein's thought on genius from the perspectives of biography and autobiography, see Immler 2011, especially ch. 6.2.
[30] Pilch 2015.   [31] Ms-104,28–64; see Pilch 2022: 59.

with the insight shared in cardinal proposition 6. The distances between the rungs of a ladder are usually the same throughout. This perspective may be difficult to uphold when actually looking at the printed pages of the *Tractatus*. But its cardinal propositions are to be seen as concatenated with each other in just the same way the links of a regular chain are concatenated, or, as for the *Tractatus,* the simple objects of an elementary state (TLP 2.03) and the simple names of an elementary proposition (TLP 4.22) are concatenated. One might well say that there is indeed *no* space between one *Tractatus* cardinal rung and the next. They 'hang one in another' (TLP 2.03; Ramsey-Ogden translation). We can also say that the rungs of the ladder are linked together by an unbroken chain that is built out of the central terms of the cardinal propositions. Also Anscombe thought that 'the *Tractatus* really does have a "natural order of advance from one topic to another, without breaks"'.[32] The structure that brings about the chain is the following: a is b, b is c, c is d and so on. The chain begins with the *world* (TLP 1) and from that leads to *what is the case* (TLP 1–2), *fact* (TLP 2–3), *thought* (TLP 3–4), *sentence* (TLP 4–5), *truth function* (TLP 5–6) and right up to 'the destination envisaged',[33] namely the culminating insight into the general form of the truth function and the proposition (TLP 6). Up to TLP 6, the term with which the cardinal proposition ends is, except for TLP 3,[34] repeated at the beginning of the next cardinal proposition, thereby making the link gapless. The link between TLP 6 and 7 is no longer as explicit as the links up to TLP 6. Nevertheless, the link is present, since what can be said and whereof one *cannot* speak (TLP 7) is determined by the general form *any* proposition can take (TLP 6) and it is only *in* language that the limit between the two can be drawn (TLP Preface).

From the printed *Tractatus* it may seem that the decimal-numbered propositions are to lead from one cardinal proposition to the next – that they are to be read *subsequently* to reading the cardinal proposition to which they adhere. But the opposite is the case – at least with regard to TLP 1.#-5.#. *Between* the cardinal propositions there is no space for additional rungs or ladders. The decimal-numbered propositions of TLP 1–5 are solely there as scaffoldings to help grasp the very cardinal proposition to which they adhere. Wittgenstein states in the footnote to TLP 1 that the decimal-numbered propositions are remarks ('Bemerkungen') or comments *on* the cardinal proposition. They relate either immediately to the cardinal proposition or to one of the other propositions relating to it. The reader is asked to climb TLP 1 first and to take as 'the world' 'everything that is the case'. But if this should be difficult to grasp, the decimal-numbered propositions have their use as auxiliaries. Taking in TLP 1.1 and 1.2

---

[32] Anscombe 1969: 374. [33] McGuinness 2002a: 277. [34] See Erbacher 2015: 68–70.

before climbing the main rung 1 may help. If in turn also TLP 1.1 should turn out to be difficult, taking in TLP 1.11–1.13 first may help. The same procedure applies regarding TLP 1.2 and so on. One may just as well start climbing the *Tractatus* by taking in the most extended decimal-numbered propositions first: for example, TLP 1.11–1.13 for moving up to TLP 1, or TLP 4.0312 (the 'Grundgedanke'-remark) for moving through TLP 4.031 to TLP 4.03, and further up to TLP 4. It is important to see that the auxiliary propositions do not add to the spaces between the rungs of the main ladder. Just as with Zeno's paradox, the space the main rung takes is not increased by zooming in on it and by treating it in smaller and smaller units. The auxiliary propositions are to be brought into play as needed by the reader. But the reader capable of reaching the insight of TLP 6 by climbing the rungs alone is not dependent on them. The reader, who already has had the same or similar thoughts as are expressed in the *Tractatus*, can do without them or needs only some of them. When reading the book, this reader will find themselves already resonating with the book's structure and contents and can thus find *pleasure* in reading it (TLP Preface).

TLP 6, sharing the insight into the general form of the truth function and the proposition, is the *climax* of the ladder. The insight is given by way of a formula and is ultimately the only insight for the reader to gain. It is both the final outcome of the book *and* the universal key to solving philosophical problems that the reader should now have in their possession. While the decimal-numbered comments on the first five cardinal propositions are auxiliaries to help grasp the latter, the comments on TLP 6 are no longer auxiliaries. They take the form of consequences *drawn* from the insight won at TLP 6 for traditional philosophy as well as the book and its author themselves. They thus provide examples of use of the key won with TLP 6. Neither are supporting comments offered on cardinal proposition 7 nor are consequences drawn from it. The explanation for this move is given in TLP 7 itself.

The *Tractatus* endorses a concept of clarification that implies *complete* clarification, that is the complete clearing away of philosophical concepts, conceptions and problems. This is only possible because it regards philosophical concepts and problems as having no substance, as nothing but cases of language being misled and misleading further. The activity of philosophical clarification is then essentially about being austere and getting rid of unnecessary, superfluous thinking and talking in philosophy itself. Wittgenstein will also later occasionally say: 'What is not required, is superfluous' (Ms-109,294). In the spring of 1932, Wittgenstein notes the following as a fitting description of his philosophy: 'I destroy, I destroy, I destroy' (CV 21/19). Paul Engelmann, one of Wittgenstein's friends, summarises Wittgenstein's early philosophy in the following words: the philosopher shall not speak 'unless it is necessary, and will then speak little' (CPE 134). Examples of useless ('unnütz') philosophical drivel ('Geschwätz') were for Wittgenstein 'If something happens it certainly can happen', 'If the body is here then there certainly must also be a space for it' (EPB 169), as well as 'the chatter about cause & effect in history books' (CV 62/71). The *Tractatus* motto states: what is to be said in philosophy shall be said 'in three words'. Wittgenstein was particularly opposed to what he called 'transcendental' drivel: 'Nur kein transzendentales Geschwätz, wenn alles so klar ist wie eine Watschen' (CPE 12). It may be tempting to read his later statement 'really one should write philosophy only as one *writes a poem*' ('dichten'; CV 24/28) in this spirit: after philosophy has said what it *can* say, there is nothing left for it to say – and what it still wants to say is better put in *poetry*. Wittgenstein regarded Uhland's poem 'Graf Eberhards Weißdorn' a 'magnificent' example (CPE 6).

Wittgenstein says in 1932 that for his work of clarification he has taken over and adapted from others specific ways of moving his thoughts ('Gedankenbewegungen'; CV 19/16). Then he lists ten sources: Boltzmann, Hertz, Schopenhauer, Frege, Russell, Kraus, Loos, Weininger, Spengler and Sraffa. He has possibly taken from Loos, the author of *Ornament and Crime*,[35] the move to treat philosophical language and concepts as ornamental surplus. This surplus of philosophical conceptions often reveals itself in the futility of arguing for them; we have no *use* for them. The strategy of bringing problematic philosophical concepts back ('zurückführen') to concepts that are, at least in the *Tractatus* view, not problematic is itself a methodological move that Wittgenstein has borrowed from others. The source of this move was most likely Frege who pioneered transforming problematic mathematical concepts into mathematical concepts that were less problematic and transforming even these into concepts and procedures of *logic*.[36] Bringing philosophy to logical analyses as safe ground is a move that Wittgenstein might have taken from Russell. Gapless sequence ('lückenlose Folge') is a method that Wittgenstein quite possibly again adopted from Frege.[37] It will accompany him throughout his philosophical authorship. In the *Investigations* Wittgenstein will use the word 'lückenlos' in two central places: in the preface ('in einer natürlichen und lückenlosen Folge') and in the discussion of family resemblance in §67 ('das lückenlose Übergreifen dieser Fasern').

Wittgenstein's philosophy is a work of clarification in two senses: one is the task of clarification as the clarifying activity that he conducts on himself, that is on his own philosophical conceptions and problems. The other is the task of forming

---

[35] Loos 1929.   [36] Frege 1884.
[37] See Frege 1884: xxi; 1893: vii–viii, x: 'Lückenlosigkeit' (1960: 138, 142).

out of these activities also a book for his readers. As a work of clarification, philosophy becomes an activity rather than a doctrine, namely: the activity of 'logical clarification of thoughts' (TLP 4.112). In the *Notes on Logic* (Ts-201a1, b21), Wittgenstein still spoke of philosophy as a doctrine. It was only from late 1915/early 1916 (Ms-104,18) onwards that he called philosophy an activity rather than a theory or doctrine ('Lehre'; TLP 4.112). Freeing oneself from misled and misleading philosophical concepts and language will let one 'see the world aright' (TLP 6.54). In this context, Wittgenstein will use a word that may seem surprising. He speaks of 'justice to the facts' ('Gerechtigkeit gegen die Tatsachen', Ms-110,184; 1931), or of 'seeing the facts without prejudice' ('die Tatsachen unparteiisch sehen'; Z §446), for our biggest difficulty is 'to take the world as it is' ('die Welt zu nehmen, wie sie ist', Ms-110,174; 1931). The aim of philosophy is hence to help re-establish justice to the world, the other, and to ourselves. By removing oneself from where language is at work, one becomes unjust; it is the task of the philosopher to first make visible and then rectify philosophy's own injustices (Ms-111,86; 1931). Seeing ourselves and the world aright is thus not only a matter of truth and truthfulness but also of justice. This perspective was possibly inspired by Kraus, who thought that any deep engagement with language eventually becomes a question of ethics. Clearing away the ornamental in places where it was superfluous was considered to be a *moral* duty also by Loos. The ethical aspect is further brought out when Wittgenstein says that work on philosophy is 'really more work on oneself' (CV 16/24). Not surprisingly, Wittgenstein thought that the sense of his *Tractatus* was an ethical one (ICE: To Ficker after 20.10.1919). It was the state of complete clarity that would again permit one to see the world aright, which he hoped his reader would achieve through the ladder form. The reader had to climb successively, rung by rung, up to the top, where they finally gain the insight. It had been the function of the ladder format to bring the reader to confront themselves with, and to process rung by rung, some of the strongest metaphysical concepts and questions philosophy has ever ploughed. All this effort of taking in philosophical language and thought had the purpose of eventually making them disappear. The ladder had the task of disencumbering the reader from philosophical surplus baggage.[38]

1.4 The Turn Away from the Ladder

By November 1930 Wittgenstein had lost interest in arranging his book for the reader in the form of a ladder: 'if the place I want to reach could only be climbed up to by a ladder, I would give up trying to get there. For the place to which I really have to go is one that I must actually be at already' (CV 7/10). Now,

---

[38] For other discussions of the *Tractatus* form, see Bazzocchi 2014 and Stern 2016.

ideally, Wittgenstein wants to offer a view of 'the whole thing' already with each single sentence (CV 7/9). In the preface to the *Investigations,* Wittgenstein will express himself in much the same way: each single remark of the book, as much as possible, shall 'give the viewer an idea of the [entire] landscape'. It should be possible to offer the reader philosophical clarification without first forcing onto them specialised philosophy, as was the case in the *Tractatus.* The place where philosophy can be left behind 'is one that I must actually be at already'. This place is language *as it is practised in everyday life* – 'our language', as Wittgenstein puts it in the summary of his new book of 1930, the *Philosophische Bemerkungen* (Ts-209,1; PR §1). The reader should no longer be forced to eliminate their philosophical ballast by first making them take in philosophical concepts, thereby trying to make the ballast more explicit and manageable. Wittgenstein now thinks that all he needs to do as the author is to offer a 'perspicuous representation' of the grammar of *everyday* language and to bring the philosopher back to it (Ts-209,1; PR §1).

Where the *Tractatus* had offered logical clarification, Wittgenstein now wants to offer 'grammatical' clarification. Where the *Tractatus* had done logical analysis, he now wants to simply give a description ('Darstellung') of the use of philosophically problematic concepts in everyday language. Where the *Tractatus* had aimed at bringing the reader to *the* ultimate insight, the insights gained now shall all be on the same level. The hope in November 1930 was that by getting an overview of philosophical language's *everyday* grammar, the reader would be enabled to make all their philosophical problems vanish on their own. They would simply *see* how philosophical concepts and thinking represent a misleading and unnecessary departure from that grammar. But the complete vanishing could not, contrary to what had been envisaged by the *Tractatus,* happen more or less in a flash. It had to happen piecemeal. Freeing oneself from philosophical problems was something that required *at least* as much effort on the reader's side as it did on the author's. The reader would have to visit 'the same thing over and over again' (CV 7/9), and to engage constantly with problems through a wide range of *different* methods (§133), rather than via the very restricted set of methods, or the *one* method only,[39] proposed in the *Tractatus.* The activity could turn out to be never-ending. For the reader to succeed, they needed guidance, support and continuous encouragement by a work of the right shape. The book had to provide leadership.

There has been discussion whether the magnum opus of the early 1930s, the *Big Typescript* (Ts-213) from 1933, should count as a philosophical work or

---

[39] Conant 2011.

rather as a collection of remarks only, even if a well-organised one.[40] It was a 'projected work' at least. The actual composition took place in Ts-212, where it is still visible in all its materiality.[41] But while it no longer will end up with either a ladder or another design in *gapless* sequence, its making still strikingly resembles the making of the *Tractatus* in many respects. It follows a method very similar to the method applied to the composition of the *Tractatus*, namely: the method of interpolation. The organisation of its contents by keywords, which later turn into chapter headings, can be compared to the organisation of the *Tractatus* contents by cardinal propositions. The chapter headings are on a par with the cardinal propositions in the *Tractatus*. The section headings are on a par with the first level decimal-numbered propositions. Finally, the actual remarks are on a par with the decimal-numbered propositions on second, third and so on levels. The *Big Typescript* chapter heading 'Understanding' could then, in analogy with the numbering of the sentences in the *Tractatus*, be numbered 1; the section heading 'Understanding, meaning, drop out of our considerations' could be numbered 1.1; and the first remark 'Can one understand . . .' could be numbered 1.1.1. In this way the position that each single remark occupies in the whole of the book and from where it can 'work in the spirit of the whole' (CV 8–9) could be made clear.

With regard to rigidity in sequence and organisation, both Ts-212 and Ts-213 can be seen to take a middle position between the ladder of the *Tractatus* and the album of the *Investigations*. Their design is different from an album of more or less 'flat' structure with no visible subdivisions at all, in as much as it is explicitly divided in chapters and sections. It is different also from a ladder inasmuch as it has much less rigidity of structure. Wittgenstein knew the advantages of a loose structure for both the author and the reader. In a remark from the spring of 1932 (Ms-154,9v-10r) Wittgenstein wonders how, in a book, he could best organise his remarks. He contemplates a maximally simple procedure by grouping the remarks through fitting keywords and then arranging the groups in the alphabetical order of the keywords. It was this classification system that had been carried out in the composition of Ts-212.[42] In the same remark from the spring of 1932 (Ms-154,9v) Wittgenstein pondered whether he should name his new work 'Philosophische Bemerkungen' rather than 'Philosophische Betrachtungen'. The first would not promise more than a book consisting of more or less single remarks, and no specific reading sequence would be suggested.

---

[40] See Uffelmann 2018: 111–5.   [41] See Krüger 1993.   [42] Rothhaupt 2010.

1.5 *Bemerkungen* and *Betrachtungen* of Perspicuous Representation

The meaning of the literary genre label 'Betrachtung' is 'consideration', 'contemplation' and 'meditation'. The *Betrachtung* is in the tradition of philosophical meditation and essay. A widely acknowledged master of this is Schopenhauer. It is characteristic of the *Betrachtung* that it opposes top down procedure and any unfitting systematisation in either content or form. It seeks instead to start from the 'intuition' of the concrete and to keep the concrete in focus. Whatever is given universal status is to emerge in the presentation from the particular.[43] The *Betrachtung* occupies a middle position between the format of '*Bemerkungen* only' on the one hand and a much stricter format like the *Abhandlung* on the other.[44]

Wittgenstein's question concerning the form his book should be given was fundamentally a question about the form perspicuous representation ('übersichtliche Darstellung'; §122) should take in it. In order to help the philosophical reader successfully return the philosophical use of words to their proper use in everyday language one needs to first offer them a 'synopsis' (LC 5:13) or 'overview' ('Übersicht'; §122) of everyday language. But everyday language is a 'labyrinth' (§203), and we continuously lack this overview. This entangles us in conceptual confusions from the beginning: philosophical confusions are 'deeply rooted in our forms of expression' (BBB 37). Taking in the perspicuous representation of the words used in the phrasing of one's philosophical problem will be the first step towards solving or dissolving (BBB 47) the philosophical problem. An overview of the depth grammar of everyday language will, by yielding clarity, have an effect on philosophy like the sun has when dispersing clouds in the sky, or like the effect 'sunlight has on the growth of potato shoots (In a dark cellar they grow yards long.)' (PG II §25).

Here we see that 'clarity' is for Wittgenstein synonymous with 'transparency' ('Durchsichtigkeit'), and the task of perspicuous representation is to eventually make the philosophical argument transparent ('durchsichtig') so that we can see the facts, especially the grammatical facts, aright (BT 306; §118).[45] Also, rigour in mathematical proof is nothing but clarity (BT 485). The German 'mit sich selbst ins Reine kommen' ('to come clean with oneself')[46] carries the same notion of clarity and transparency, but stresses the ethical aspect even more. The philosopher is therefore called upon to begin their true task by working on an

---

[43] Cerný 1972: 747.   [44] See also Pichler 2013b, Pichler 2016 and Zambito (forthcoming).
[45] See also BBB 17; CV 7/9, 9/12; PR Foreword (Ms-109,211); Ms-108,291; Ms-113,33r; Ms-114,30r; Ms-131,202 and Ms-134,28–29.
[46] ICE: To Russell probably Christmas 1913; see also Ms-134,143.

overview of language and its concepts through perspicuous representation of it. Perspicuous representation helps us regain control over our concepts. With it in place, we can, first, recognise our false assumptions about grammar, ourselves and the world, and, second, clear up our conceptual misunderstandings. Early Wittgenstein had thought that philosophy could achieve this control by providing the correct *logical* analysis of language. The Wittgenstein of the *Blue* and *Brown Book*s thinks that giving a clear arrangement, a perspicuous representation of language as it is used in functional *everyday* scenarios, is the correct means to produce the overview. These scenarios could be real or invented. Philosophy is to be returned to everyday language: 'What *we* do is to bring words back from their metaphysical to their everyday use' (§116). One must, however, be careful in attributing such a position to the later Wittgenstein generally.[47]

The question what form perspicuous representation should take in the book became for Wittgenstein very much a question about *how much* guidance and leadership should be provided to the reader. Should there be a division into sections with headings like in the *Big Typescript*? Should there be 'free-wheeling discourse'[48] or rather linear progression? Should the remarks simply be collected under alphabetically ordered keyword headings? How should the book start? To what extent should the author make his thoughts on the form of the book explicit? These and similar questions also charged the Wittgenstein–Waismann project. Waismann had in the early 1930s entered into a cooperation with Wittgenstein to assist him in authoring a book presenting his philosophy. This was on the initiative of Schlick.[49] Waismann soon recognised that the project was far from straightforward. The issue of how to *begin* the book became of particular concern. On the basis of manuscripts and dictations by Wittgenstein, Waismann produced a first draft. But at a meeting at Easter 1933, Wittgenstein laid out a new vision for its composition, namely: the later *Brown Book*'s format.[50]

1.6 The *Brown Book* Gapless Series of Language-Games

In the *Brown Book*, Wittgenstein offers the reader a perspicuous representation of the grammar of those parts of everyday language that are most relevant to the philosopher. Nouns, proper names, demonstratives, indexicals and numerals are examples. Philosophical thought should be shown to be redundant by demonstrating that its concepts and phrasings simply have no place in the grammar of

---

[47] See also Stern 2004: 125–32.   [48] Perloff 2011: 720.
[49] See McGuinness' preface to WWK and McGuinness and Baker's 'Nachwort' in Waismann 1976.
[50] See Waismann's letter to Schlick 9.8.1934 (Iven 2015: 160–2) and to Menger from 1936 (Manninen 2011: 20).

everyday language, and all that philosophy does is to deviate from it. Naturally, we all deviate from everyday use of words or 'grammar' (§29 *et passim*), and doing so can be a mark of *poetry*, for example in funny literature for children (and adults) such as Carroll's *Alice in Wonderland*. What, according to the preceding *Blue Book*, makes philosophy special is that it, rather than having a good laugh over such literature's grammatical jokes and then *returning* itself to everyday language, cultivates the deviation from it. It lets itself be *mystified* by puzzling language use and mystifies it further by reification of the puzzling concept, for example of 'time' as an object (BBB 6). Wittgenstein thinks that 'philosophers are often like little children who first scribble some marks on a piece of paper at random and now ask the grown-up "what's that?"' (CV 17/24).

Philosophers have traditionally dealt with questions such as 'What is meaning?', 'What is truth?', 'What is rule-following?', 'What is a fact?', 'What is knowledge?', 'Is the inner private?', 'What is thinking?', 'Can there be thinking without language?' and 'What is language?' by defining the concepts that feature in the question, or at the very least by analysing the question into its components. In contrast to the traditional 'What is . . . ?'-method, Wittgenstein in the *Blue* and *Brown Books* proposes to approach the issue through his language-game method which was first introduced in 1931. This method asks us to find simple cases of language use, that is language-games where the terms configuring the philosophical question are used in unproblematic ways. 'When we look at such simple forms of language, the mental mist which seems to enshroud our ordinary use of language disappears' (BBB 17). Wittgenstein's language-games can occur in actual everyday language, or they can be fictive, invented, 'improvisational exercises'.[51] Philosophers (as well as linguists) may want to define language along a number of functions, including representation, expression, appeal, phatic use and so on. But Wittgenstein argues that the very simple use of words by the two builders from §2, even if it is only the use of four nouns, is already *language*. For it is the use of words as serving to coordinate an interaction between two people and, thus most importantly, it is interwoven with *acting* and is acting itself.

The language-game method starts by identifying in the philosophical problem the words and concepts that are problematic. From there it can play out in a number of ways. But they all involve methodological comparison with a situation where language use is intertwined with *acting* in a supposedly unproblematic way. The intertwining of language with action is the principal characteristic of a language-game (§7); a mere play with words is thus no

---

[51] Savickey 2017: xvi.

language-game in Wittgenstein's sense. Two prominent versions of the method involve comparison with a language-game that either *contrasts* or, respectively, *conforms* with the philosophically problematic use. The first, that is the contrast-oriented version, is exemplified by the shopping example in §1: the philosophically problematic concept in question is the concept of meaning. The context of action, the language-game, within which the concept of meaning does its work and to which the problematic use of 'meaning' shall be compared, is the situation of buying five red apples (without the word 'meaning' itself ever being used). The guiding question is: how *different* is the philosophical concept of meaning – 'meaning is reference' – from the concept of meaning as it is in play in the language-game of the shopping example? The result of the comparison – meaning is much more than reference, and it is *humans* who refer not words – should make the philosopher, who wants to maintain that meaning is reference, think twice.

The second, initially confirmation-oriented version (called 'the method of §2' in §48) is exemplified by the builders' language-game. The philosophically problematic concept in question is here, again, the concept of meaning. The context of action, the language-game, within which this concept does its work, and to which the philosophically problematic use of 'meaning' shall be compared, is the situation of two people erecting a building. The guiding question is now: how *representative* is the concept of meaning as it is in play in the builders' language-game for the *entire*, actually existing, language-game of 'meaning'? Naturally, the answer to the question is: not at all.

Similar simple language-game scenarios can be developed for 'truth', 'rule', 'knowledge', 'simple', 'thinking', 'understanding' as also for other concepts entering philosophical conceptions and problems. The concept of the game entails that no move stands alone. There is no move in a game that comes without another move or does not lead to other moves. These other moves can take the form of language or also extralingual action and behaviour. The insight that moves in language are not without connection to moves in action and activity proves fruitful for treating a number of philosophical issues, for example philosophical thought about belief. Wittgenstein contends that it is a mistake to treat belief as a solely epistemological affair. Rather, belief comes with specific consequences and actions. An area where later Wittgenstein put this view to work is religious belief (see LA 53–71).[52]

In the *Brown Book* then, Wittgenstein seeks to return the philosophically problematic handling of words, concepts and distinctions to where they belong and are not problematic, namely: the contexts of their learning and use in

---

[52] See also Stern 2004: 10–5.

language-games.[53] Its language-games deal (1) with nouns, (2) with numerals, (3) with proper names, (4) with indexicals and adverbs, (5) with question and answer, (6) with asking for a name, (7) with correlating words and pictures/tables, (8) with distinguishing sentence and word, (9) with word order and distinguishing type and tokens, (10) with ordinals and so on. Not insignificantly, Wittgenstein wanted the arrangement of these language-games to proceed in a linear and gapless sequence: the presentation should ideally leave *no gaps* in the progression from one language-game to the other, and ideally proceed from the grammar of the simplest case (nouns) to the grammar of the most complex one. This strategy for doing perspicuous representation for the reader conformed again with the Fregean method of gapless series.

As soon as Wittgenstein, in the autumn of 1934, thought that he had, with the *Brown Book*, finally found the right way to fulfil the vision presented to Waismann at Easter 1933, he let him know that their efforts and work on other formats were a thing of the past. It is hardly surprising that Waismann was disappointed.

1.7 From the *Brown Book* to the Album of the *Investigations*

At the beginning of November 1936, in Skjolden in Norway, the new form that had emerged with the *Brown Book* was itself discarded (Ms-115,292).[54] Wittgenstein told Moore that he had been pursuing the wrong method in the *Brown Book* (EPB 12–3). This method had included pairing the perspicuous representation with an ideally gapless series of language-games. By way of a linear sequence, each language-game following the previous one ideally by way of an 'extension' (BBB 79), the *Brown Book* wanted to illuminate step by step and one after the other all fields of grammar relevant to philosophy. 'According to the role which propositions play in a language-game', distinctions between different kinds of propositions were introduced: 'orders, questions, explanations, descriptions, & so on' (BBB 82). The *Brown Book*'s linear sequence starts with the builders' game that introduces naming and demonstrative teaching. Then it goes on with an extension of the game, introducing, in addition to demonstrative teaching, learning numerals by heart, pointing and gesture. In the third game, pronouncing and working with proper names are introduced. And so forth. For each new game, Wittgenstein elaborates how what looks like the same function of language can work differently in a new context. In this way, the single language-games provide 'objects of comparison' (§130)

---

[53] Note that the *Brown Book* items in the Skinner archives exceed the version published by Rhees (Ts-310); see Gibson's comments in DPS 25–9, 75–6 and 86–7, as well as the edition of the twenty-eight page extension in Skinner's hand in DPS ch. 4.

[54] For details, see Pichler 2004 and 2007: 137–9.

for the philosopher, and as such they invite general reflections and objections that are interpolated and dealt with in between them. At several places, Wittgenstein acknowledges that related topics are knocking at the door, though it is not yet 'their turn' to participate in the discussions. Their treatment is postponed or dropped. For one of the mottos of the *Brown Book* was: don't deviate from the linear presentation. First do a, then do b, then do c and so on, and don't do c before you have done b. It will come as no surprise that Wittgenstein in the end found the *Brown Book* project of the *gapless linear series of language-games*, if not impossible and in parts very arbitrary, 'boring & artificial' (ICE: To Moore 20.11.1936).

The series format of the *Brown Book* had kept Wittgenstein pleased for two years from the autumn of 1934 to the autumn of 1936. Then he realised that it was 'worthless' (Ms-115,292). He now thinks that the linear and gapless order was not 'natural' in two important senses: first, it was not natural to him as a thinker, a writer and an author. In September 1937, Wittgenstein observes: 'If I am thinking just for myself without wanting to write a book, I jump about all round the topic; that is the only way of thinking that is *natural* to me' (CV 28/33; my italics). And he goes on to lament that he is wasting 'untold effort making an arrangement of my thoughts that may have no value whatever' (CV 28/33). Second, it was not natural to philosophy either (Preface).

It is telling that for the *Investigations*, Wittgenstein decided to respect the form in which the contents of the book had originally been produced, namely: as *remarks*. He *could* have tried to compose them into a more linear and strongly sequential work as he had done in the *Tractatus* and the *Brown Book*. But he did not do so. Here we see that it is critical to distinguish between, on the one hand, stylistic and form features being present in the first writing of remarks, and, on the other, possibly the same features becoming characteristics of works *by composition*.[55] The fact that the form of the first writing and the form of the composed work differ where they differ (as in the case of the *Tractatus*) shows us that attention to the form of the resulting work is important. So does the fact of their convergence where they do converge, as in the case of the *Investigations*. The genesis of the *Tractatus*, the *Big Typescript* and of the *Investigations*, as they manifest themselves in the *Nachlass*, all show striking similarities, but the end results for each are radically different with regard to work form. These are aspects whose importance can be adequately appreciated only if one at the very outset draws a distinction between first writing of philosophical remarks on the one hand and their composition into works for the reader on the other.[56]

---

[55] Pichler 2013b: 70. [56] See Section 1.1.

With the *Brown Book* Wittgenstein had wanted to do something more than provide the 'mirror in which my reader sees his own thinking with all its deformities & with this assistance can set it in order' (CV 18/25), yet at the same time he had also wanted to do something less. He had wanted to do less because he wanted only to mirror non-philosophical everyday grammar, but the book for the reader was eventually to also mirror the philosophical deformations themselves. He had wanted to do more because he wanted the *Brown Book* to be more than just a mirror. It was to be a tutorial. With the *Investigations* he wanted to resolve both deficiencies. Moreover, choosing the form that was not only natural to the philosophical investigation but also to his preferred writing style was also a point of honesty and confession for Wittgenstein: it is the *authentic* writing self of the author that shall shine through in the form of the book.[57] As in 1930, when Wittgenstein distanced himself from the gapless *Tractatus* ladder, he now returned to a less rigid form of working out the perspicuous representation. This form was the criss-cross form of the album.

At the beginning of November 1936, the *Brown Book* was turned into the album of the *Investigations*. However, it would only be much later in 1946 that Wittgenstein also *called* his *Investigations* an 'album' (Ms-130,22). We should keep in mind though that already fifteen years earlier, with his 'preface' remarks from November 1930 (CV 6–8/8–11), he had masterfully described and announced it.

2 Methods for the Apt Movement of Thought

2.1 Ten Masters

In a remark from the spring of 1932 (Ms-154,15v-16r, published in CV 18–9/16), Wittgenstein says that none of the 'Gedankenbewegungen', which he uses for his philosophical work of clarification ('Klärungswerk'), had been invented by himself, but was always adopted from someone else. Then he gives the list of the ten people already cited.[58] Originally, the list only contained 'Frege, Russell, Spengler, Sraffa'. The systematic study of the influences exerted by these ten figures on Wittgenstein was first carried out by Janik (2006).

The list reveals a remarkably diverse group of scholars. Boltzmann was a severe critic of speculative philosophy, and one of the key representatives of such philosophy was, in Boltzmann's eyes, Schopenhauer. Frege defended Platonism about truth and the laws of logic; Weininger defended generalities, 'ideal types' and their principal dichotomies. In contrast stands Sraffa, the pragmatist, who with a simple Neapolitan gesture would bring Wittgenstein to

---

[57] See Pichler 2013b and 2016. [58] See page 13.

accept that 'we should give up the generalities and take particular cases, from which we started' (WC 196).[59] Schopenhauer wanted to base ethics on compassion while Weininger defended the Kantian approach of duty and in particular the idea of duty to oneself. Frege was an author of remarkably gapless and rigid logical discourses; in this respect he presents a contrast to Kraus, the author of a magnum opus that consists of only loosely connected theatrical scenes. Scientistic Russell contrasts with anti-scientistic Spengler. Spengler was in parts a cultural relativist, while Russell and Frege were protagonists of realism. Spengler was also a defender of a dichotomy between the realm of science on the one hand and the realm of history, culture and the human on the other; Weininger, on the other hand, sought to put into a mathematical formula the observed general form of sexual attraction between male and female.

Here we see great opposites. It is as though Wittgenstein wants to tell us that philosophy needs to learn and draw from a huge variety of thinkers as diverse as those ten figures. The success of philosophy depends on jointly representing a full variety and spectrum of diverse approaches in spite of real or actual contradictions implied by them. At least he seems to think that this is what his own work in philosophy needs.

2.2 Movements of Thought

What does Wittgenstein mean by 'Gedankenbewegung' – literally 'movement of thought(s)'? Let us look at some other places where he uses this expression. In a remark from early 1931 (Ms-109,291–2), Freud's move to declare as (manifest) dream what is *reported* as the dream is labelled with this word. In April 1938 (Ms-120,145r), Wittgenstein describes his project not as one that teaches thinking that is *more correct*, but as one that teaches a different and new 'Gedankenbewegung': a new way of moving one's thought. This he recognises as a project of Nietzschean transvaluation ('Umwertung'), and he relates it to his view that the philosopher should be a *poet*. In the spring of 1944 (Ms-124,150; see variant in Ms-127,91–2), he calls the following reasoning an *important* movement of thought: in order to recognise a specific reaction as X, one has to see it in the context of specific forms of life and language, just as one needs to see a facial expression as belonging to a face in order to recognise it as a specific facial expression. Some six years prior to this, Wittgenstein said that a language-game is one only in the context of a whole culture (LA 8). In December 1947 (CV 64/73–4), Wittgenstein laments that most of our movements of thought are caught from others – that they have become standards and beaten tracks to which one has become habituated. What we need instead is

---

[59] See Engelmann 2013: 151–60.

original *new* ways of going from one thought to another. Many of our traditional ways are, he thinks, completely useless (at least for philosophical clarification), and it is important that our movement of thought as such becomes clarified. Finally, in a remark from the summer of 1948 (Ms-137,47b), Wittgenstein calls the questions 'Why should ... ' and 'Why shouldn't ... ' *philosophical* movements of thought.

While it may well be that some of the occurrences of 'Denkbewegung' (e.g. CV 20/17) also belong with 'movement of thought',[60] Wittgenstein's uses of 'Gedankenbewegung' show that it has to be distinguished from 'thought' ('Gedanke') and 'way of thinking' ('Denkweise'). What is primarily meant by the expression is the specific *way* in which one *gets on* with a thought, an idea, a concept, a perspective, a philosophical approach, rather than the general idea, concept, perspective or philosophical approach itself. This fits with a remark made in April 1942 where Wittgenstein stresses the great extent to which Spengler influences him in his activity of thinking.[61] It thus refers to procedures, moves and strategies for one's thinking, talking and writing – *methods* for bringing about the right transition from one thought to another, from one remark to another, from one sentence to another, as also from one word to another. Continuing with an explanation, a question, making an inference, suggesting an alternative way of presenting the matter, coming up with a comparison, an example, an analogy or simile ('Gleichnis') are all considered ways of moving one's thought. Rhees gave an example of a typical Wittgensteinian move when he reported in 1933: 'If something does not become clear, he does not try to give an explanation in simple words but instead looks for a new simile [*Gleichnis*]'. Rhees regarded this as one of Wittgenstein's *methods*.[62] 'A good simile refreshes the intellect' (CV 1/3) and helps to see things in entirely new ways. This is decisive, not least when being stuck with a philosophical problem. Wittgenstein thought that he was capable of inventing new helpful similes (CV 19/16); at the same time, he sorely missed this capacity in other philosophers, for example F. P. Ramsey (Ms-106,110; 1929). He also thought he was the inventor of certain artifices ('Kunstgriffe') that help clarify a discussion, and thus comparable to someone who invents new, more surveyable ('übersichtlichere') ways of accounting (Ms-135,74r; 1947). He sees a connection between this activity and mathematics.

Making the right move is important also *within* sentences and comes for Wittgenstein not only with the right wording but also felicitous stress through

---

[60] Klagge 2021: 204.
[61] Ms-125,30v; the wording is '*bei* meinem Denken', not '*in* meinem Denken' (my italics). See also Haller 1988: 78, 119.
[62] Rhees to Kastil 5.11.1933, cited after Erbacher et al. 2019: 118.

underlining (spacing in typescripts) and use of punctuation for appropriate intonation, rhythm and pausing. Comma, semicolon, colon, dash, double dash or parentheses are in this context frequently considered alternatives, each having their own specific effect.[63] Wittgenstein's labour on getting the wording and the prosody right may well have been guided by Goethe and Spengler's thought that one and the same phenomenon can be represented in radically different ways.[64] Hertz showed the importance of providing alternative representations and orderings of knowledge.[65] To Gilpatric Wittgenstein said in 1951 'that he had a large number of manuscripts which showed the traces of constant refinement in expression. In many cases he had tried to express the same point in several different ways. Now he does not feel competent to choose which among alternatives is the better formulation'.[66]

Sometimes Wittgenstein laments not being able to bring his thoughts adequately to the surface, sustain their right motion and tempo, permit them calm progression, prevent them from breaking off as soon as they finally got properly going.[67] The apt movement of thought is the apt method for moving the activity of philosophical clarification forward efficiently. This includes methods for shaping the precipitate from these activities to an apt presentation for the reader. 'Gedankenbewegung' can be natural or learned, spontaneous or willed. People can differ strongly in their ways of thought movement – as Wittgenstein actually thought was the case with him and Sraffa: 'there can be nothing more different than your interests & mine, & your *movements of thought* & mine'.[68] Sraffa said:

> As to the method of our discussions (remarks or arguments) I have this to say. I must have long stories, not short ones; I must try to stick to a point & not saunter from one to the other, apparently disconnected; I am much too slow for that, and cannot find the hidden connection. Also I cannot be content with hints or allusions (or things which cannot be laid down black or white), I must have it all thrashed out.[69]

In addition to differences in movement of thought, it may be that Wittgenstein's adherence to (Spenglerian) 'historicism *without history*'[70] was one of the topics of dispute and led eventually to the termination of the conversations between Wittgenstein and Sraffa.[71] In contrast, Wittgenstein felt a great intellectual

---

[63] But cf. Perloff 2004: 36.   [64] Schulte 1990: 34.   [65] Janik 2006: ch. 2.
[66] Leach 2020: 214.   [67] See Ms-118,8v and 37r, Ms-119,109v, Ms-157a,61v, Ms-183,161.
[68] To Sraffa 23.8.1949 (WC 450; my italics). See also '... the difficulty to understand each other when the natural *movements of thought* are different' (To Sraffa 21.2.1934, in De Iaco 2019: 217; my italics).
[69] WC: 227; see also De Iaco 2019: 211–3.   [70] Hacker 2013: 117.
[71] De Iaco 2019: 214; Mazzeo 2021: ch. 1. De Iaco 2018 provides a list of meetings between Wittgenstein and Sraffa.

affinity to Loos, and in the early days of their acquaintance Loos had said to Wittgenstein: 'You are me!' (CPE 127).

2.3 What about Ramsey and Others?

The list of the ten figures from whom Wittgenstein adopted (and adapted) ways of moving his thought, 'Gedankenbewegung', is most likely meant to be chronological.[72] But saying this leaves it open whether the chronology concerns the time of acquaintance with the thinker, or alternatively the moment of influence, or even when the influence was properly put to work. Another open question is why we don't seem to find on the list other figures we think influenced Wittgenstein. We don't need to go to writers who became mostly relevant to Wittgenstein only *post* 1932, for example Köhler and Newman. There are plenty of influential figures available before 1932, who are *not* on the list. Examples are Augustine, Nietzsche, Kierkegaard, Tolstoy, James, Mauthner, Freud, Ernst, Ramsey, Brouwer, and possibly also Malinowski.[73] Another case is Wittgenstein's school teacher, a certain Groag (possibly Jonas Groag) whom Wittgenstein explicitly acknowledges in the very same spring of 1932 (Ms-113,51v) as the one from whom he, in his own words, learned to begin a grammatical investigation ('sprachliche Betrachtung') with a group of examples.

I think the second question – why we don't also find these and other influential figures on the list – can be addressed as follows. First of all, Wittgenstein doesn't say that the list is complete, though it may well be the case. If according to Wittgenstein the list *is* complete, the answer must further include the following: while all these figures might have been hugely important influences, Wittgenstein apparently didn't think that they influenced him with ways of moving his thought. Note that Wittgenstein says: '*That* is how ... have influenced me' (CV 19/16; my italics). These figures then simply did not influence him *in the way* of giving him 'Gedankenbewegungen' that he would use in his philosophical work of clarification.

The absence of Ramsey on the list – with whom Wittgenstein had regular meetings in 1929 and whom Wittgenstein explicitly *acknowledges* in the preface to the *Investigations* for valuable discussions and critique – may seem particularly odd. Wittgenstein was greatly indebted to Ramsey for new ideas, approaches and critique. Particularly important was the stimulus to bring the human adequately into his philosophy of language. Wittgenstein's method in

---

[72] von Wright 1982: 213; McGuinness 1988: 37 and Janik 2006: 146, *et passim*.
[73] See Biesenbach 2014; regarding Malinowski see Nyíri 1992: 105; Engelmann 2013: 295 and Brusotti 2018.

the *Tractatus* had according to Ramsey been to 'construct a logic, and do all our philosophical analysis entirely *unselfconsciously*, thinking all the time of the facts and not about our thinking about them, deciding what we meant without any reference to the nature of meanings'.[74] Wittgenstein would still in the summer of 1929 complain that Ramsey did not understand the value he himself placed on *notation*, 'because he does not see that in it an entire way of looking at the object is expressed; the angle from which I now regard the thing. The notation is the last expression of a philosophical view'.[75] Wittgenstein's idea then was that correct notation would sufficiently mirror both the world and our view of it, and therefore, that, to see the world aright, there was no need to bring in a human that was 'self-conscious' of *their* part in representing the world. Under the influence of Ramsey, Wittgenstein will abandon this idea and think instead that it is human practices, more precisely human practices *in context*, rather than notation and grammar that represent the world and bring together world, language and thought. With the change to positive attention to human acting, new key concepts such as language-game and form of life emerge, as well as new forms of argument. One such argument is the appeal to how a word that is problematic in philosophy is used in functional everyday language and acting. Ramsey, with his emphasis on 'human logic',[76] can be regarded as formative for Wittgenstein's 'anthropological' turn. However, Wittgenstein did not seem to think that he got any specific way of *thought movement* from Ramsey that he put to work in his work of clarification. He felt that Ramsey's criticism, rather than moving his thought forward, 'didn't help along but held back and sobered' (MT 15).

2.4 Boltzmann, Hertz, Schopenhauer, Frege, Russell, Kraus, Loos, Weininger, Spengler, Sraffa

To understand Wittgenstein's philosophy and philosophical methods it is therefore important to understand the 'Gedankenbewegungen' that he received from the listed ten figures, and to connect with each figure the 'Gedankenbewegung(en)' that Wittgenstein took over. The following are some suggestions, intended as complementary to Janik's work. Hertz demonstrated the importance of working with models (including tangible models) and certainly inspired Wittgenstein's thinking about and thinking in pictures as well as his 'mature concept of philosophy'.[77] Boltzmann shared Hertz' faith in models, and like Hertz he believed that the laws and mechanisms of physics could best be regarded as pictures and analogies. Boltzmann believed that

---

[74] Ramsey 1990: 5.   [75] Translation from Misak 2016: 252.   [76] Misak 2016: 232.
[77] Janik 2006: 46.

between fields that seem far apart, 'the most surprising' structural analogies and similarities may occur.[78] Moreover, Boltzmann taught that it is highly fruitful for one's research to work closely with models, instead of relying only on hypotheses and their verification or falsification. When presenting his research results to the public, he was not afraid of bringing in thought experiments. Boltzmann himself acknowledges Maxwell and Faraday as people who strongly influenced and encouraged his use of pictures and analogies. In more than one place, Wittgenstein states that the sense of a proposition is much more similar to the meaning of, or the understanding of a melody or musical theme, than one would think (e.g. §527). Already the early Wittgenstein sees many similarities between language and music (e.g. NB 7.2.1915).[79] This is an illuminating example of putting to work Boltzmann's idea that the same structure may obtain in what appears to be quite different areas. The same is the case when Wittgenstein pictures our language as an old, but continuously growing city (§18); Wittgenstein might have got this *directly* from Boltzmann.[80] In both cases, a shared or similar structure is revealed through a pictorial relation. Boltzmann's abundant uses of pictures, comparisons, analogies and similes were surely in themselves a great inspiration and encouragement. Wittgenstein writes that what *he* invents 'are new *comparisons* [*Gleichnisse*]' (CV 19/16); that his strength consists in 'imagination' (Ms-162b,22r; 1939) and 'seeing analogies there, where one doesn't usually see them' (Ms-131,221; 1946).[81] For *the move to compare* he might have felt deeply indebted to Boltzmann – but the comparison of the sense of a proposition to the meaning of a melody might have been authentically *his*. Wittgenstein's use of 'intermediate cases' was 'fully in the spirit of Boltzmann'.[82] When supporting his clarifications with graphical illustrations such as drawings and diagrams, Wittgenstein might have taken over yet another pictorial move from Boltzmann.

Furthermore, Boltzmann vigorously showed how an apparently nonsensical philosophical statement can be put right by a grammatical remark. A case in point is the grammar of 'being of value'. Boltzmann thinks that the question whether life itself is of value and to whom and to what is simply ungrammatical ('vollkommen widersinnig'); 'being of value' simply means being of value to *life*.[83] In §50, when discussing the standard metre, Wittgenstein treats a similar case. Boltzmann had an impressive gift of supporting his critique of others with great wit, irony, sarcasm and exaggeration.[84] Responding with wit is certainly

---

[78] Boltzmann 1979: 22.   [79] See also Appelqvist 2018: 220–3.   [80] Janik 2006: 38.
[81] See also Perloff 2011: 723; Erbacher 2015: 95; Savickey 2017; Uffelmann 2018: ch. 3 and Klagge 2021: ch. 6.
[82] Janik 2006: 31.   [83] Janik 2006: 254–5.
[84] See 'Über eine These Schopenhauers' in Boltzmann 1979.

not lost on Wittgenstein's clarifications as revealed, for example, in §693. Even the German title of the *Tractatus* may contain an ironic second sense: the book trades philosophy away ('abhandeln').[85] There may be a deep connection between Wittgenstein's philosophical concern with nonsense and his personal fondness for jokes and humour that found expression in his 'Nonsense' collection.[86] Moreover, Boltzmann was a teacher in the use of examples.[87] He was also a master of using quotations – as well as of *mis-using* them for his purposes of critique. Wittgenstein used the same methods of extrapolation, exaggeration and exploitation of a citation, for example for a reductio ad absurdum. So did Frege, Loos and Kraus.

Kraus employed specific techniques of 'taking his victim "at his word", that is, of driving home his accusations and exposing threadbare intentions by the simple means of citing the accused's own words and phrases' (CPE 124). Engelmann adds that Kraus would 'conceive and express an argument only with reference to particular individuals'. Both points apply also to Wittgenstein. Even if he did not always mention the other by name, Wittgenstein often tried to address his philosophical clarification to a concrete philosophical adversary or conversation partner, for example Socrates, Plato, Augustine, Descartes, Frege, Russell, Carnap, Frazer, James, Gödel, Köhler and Moore. It may well be that the entire Appendix III of RFM I can be read as Wittgenstein discussing with Gödel.[88] In §1, Wittgenstein made Augustine a strawman for polemics with his earlier *Tractatus* self. It should be recognised that Wittgenstein does not necessarily care about interpreting the words of the adversary in the way the adversary meant them, be the adversary another thinker or another philosophical self of Wittgenstein.[89] Rather, he seeks to give the words a meaning and use that suit the particular purpose of his context. Here again, a good example is the tendentious use Wittgenstein makes of Augustine's description of how he learned language, reading into it 'Augustine's picture'.[90]

Boltzmann, Weininger and Spengler thought that the most striking analogies and similarities can occur between fields that seem far apart. For his investigation of the 'laws' of human sexual attraction, Weininger draws heavily on finding analogies in remote areas, including inorganic chemistry.[91] Weininger undertook in his *Sex and Character*, just as Wittgenstein did for philosophy, a clarification of problematic concepts: the concepts that most interested Weininger were the concept of the *male* and the concept of the *female*. He made it his task to clear up the alleged faultiness[92] of the two concepts. To this purpose he developed

---

[85] McGuinness 2006a: 373.   [86] McGuinness 2006b; see also Savickey 2017: xvi, 5–6.
[87] Boltzmann 1979: 254: 'Noch ein Beispiel ...'.   [88] Kienzler and Sunday Grève 2016.
[89] See Pichler 2007: 128–9 and 2013a: 444–5.   [90] See Baker and Hacker 2005a: ch. 1.
[91] Weininger 1904: Erster Teil, Kap. III.   [92] Weininger 1904: 7: 'Mangelhaftigkeit'.

a principal dichotomy between the type of the male (M) and the type of the female (F). According to Weininger, this dichotomy informs all natural and cultural manifestations of mankind. At the same time, the two types are not found in reality. Rather, they are only limiting 'ideal cases', 'ideas' within the scope of which we encounter the innumerable hybrid forms and intermediate cases of actual males and females. Weininger's ultimate aim is to reduce ('zurückführen') the dichotomy to a single principle, namely: the principle of sexual intermediate forms. Two areas of particular focus are genius and Jewishness that are again treated as ideal types that exist in reality as innumerable hybrid forms and intermediate cases of M and F.[93] It was a central tactic of Weininger, as of Wittgenstein, to follow ideas through 'to their ultimate consequence'.[94]

Wittgenstein found that Weininger's belief in ideal types and their radical opposition, as well as his belief in the power of stable and precise theoretical constructs, were illegitimate. It is a move least permitted in philosophy, where according to later Wittgenstein, one should not use such types even for *talking* about things, irrespective of whether one believes the types depict reality or are merely constructions (as it was in Weininger's case). The only acceptable use of ideal types is as 'objects of comparison' (§122). Wittgenstein took from his reading of Weininger the experience of the hazard of false generalisations, and therefore developed methods for trying to avoid them. Weininger had a strong tendency to generalise and exaggerate, and therefore ran the risk of making his mistakes *big* mistakes. Generalisation in philosophy is, according to Wittgenstein, one of the main sources and bearers of philosophical confusion. After reading Weininger, whenever Wittgenstein was faced with an actual or potential use of ideal types or a reduction to single principles and principal[95] dichotomies, he was wary of the pitfalls and strongly opposed such manoeuvres. Weininger himself sometimes responds to a *big* mistake by trying to pursue its opposite. Wittgenstein applies this move to Weininger's book itself: 'that is roughly speaking if you just add a "~" to the whole book it says an important truth' (ICE: To Moore 23.8.1931).

While being critical of Weininger, Wittgenstein considered him to be 'a remarkable genius' (MDN 91). In his letter to Moore he called both Weininger and his 'enormous mistake' *great* – 'great' (or, in German, 'groß') being a label that Wittgenstein *reserved* almost only for the genius (CV 9/12, 15/23, 25/29, 37–8/43, -/53). Weininger's book not only entailed strong criticism of society but also laid the grounds for deep self-criticism and persevering

---

[93] For example, Weininger 1904: Erster Teil, Kap. I, *et passim*: 'Prinzip der (sexuellen) Zwischenformen'; see also 424, 452–3.
[94] Haller 1988: 93.
[95] See the German subtitle of Weininger's book: 'Eine *prinzipielle* Untersuchung' (my italics).

self-improvement: one has, first of all, a duty to oneself – the duty of being truthful, pure, faithful and honest with oneself.[96] In Wittgenstein too we find that self-critique becomes a strength to nurture. 'You write [truly] about yourself from your own height. Here you don't stand on stilts or on a ladder but on your bare feet' (CV 33/38) invokes again the *ladder* imagery. With his persistent critique of his own former or current philosophical selves, Wittgenstein put to work Weininger's principle of uncompromising self-criticism and ethics of duty to oneself. It was possibly in this way that Weininger exhibited the strongest influence on Wittgenstein.

In the proto-version of §122, it is not Weininger but Spengler who was explicitly targeted as a proponent of 'ideal types'.[97] From Spengler (and Goethe) Wittgenstein adapted the 'morphological method'.[98] This method is geared towards seeing *forms* through comparison. For Spengler, culture, history and philosophy are 'organisms'.[99] Consequently, they require 'organic' rather than 'mechanistic' treatment: 'The means whereby to identify dead forms is Mathematical Law. The means whereby to understand living forms is Analogy.'[100] Morphological method opens up for seeing the homologous and analogous forms of cultures and phases in world history.[101] A word important to both Spengler and Wittgenstein is 'physiognomy';[102] Wittgenstein's phrase 'Meaning – a physiognomy' (§568) evokes Spengler. The forms that are compared by Spengler and Wittgenstein are 'deep' forms, not superficial ones. This attention to depth structure permits Wittgenstein to see the similarity between 'I know' and 'I am able to', or between understanding a theme in music and understanding a sentence. Eventually, comparative morphological method can be seen to be at work also in Wittgenstein's ethnological procedure, making him turn to societies or cultures with practices and meanings very different from ours.

In order to use morphological method to the fullest, one must, according to Spengler, go beyond thinking in terms of the principle of causality.[103] Philosophy is 'irresistibly tempted to ask and answer questions in the way science does' (BBB 27). Keeping Spengler's polarisation between the causal approach, on the one hand, and the 'organic' or 'historical' approach, on the other, on his mind must have made it less likely for Wittgenstein to succumb to the temptations of scientism. While in the natural sciences it makes sense to let causal explanation always continue to lower levels, Spengler probably brought

---

[96] Weininger 1904: 200, 206–7, 231.
[97] Ms-142,110–11; see also Ms-111,119 and Ms-157b,16r–16v. [98] Schulte 1992: 81–2.
[99] Spengler 1927: 104. [100] Spengler 1927: 4.
[101] Spengler 1927: ch. III–IV (1920: ch. II).
[102] For passages in Spengler, see for example 1927: ch. III (1920: ch. II).
[103] Spengler 1927: 8; see also TLP 5.1361.

Wittgenstein to stop the philosophical investigation at the level of 'protophenomena', and to accept, for example, the language-game as a *given*.[104]

According to Spengler, philosophy should follow the methods of 'comparative morphology'.[105] While Spengler remains unclear about its details, the employment of pictures, analogies, comparisons and similes seem to be central elements. *That* there could be, as Spengler promises, a *method* for using pictures, analogies, comparisons, similes and the like, rather than that these result only from 'simple inclination'[106], must in itself already have fascinated Wittgenstein and left its mark on him. Moreover, we can assume that for his work of clarification, Wittgenstein's willingness to leave behind procedures that are solely driven by 'law' and 'systematic' parameters[107] was encouraged and inspired by Spengler. Spengler finds the morphological method developed to the fullest by the *poet* ('Dichter'), especially Goethe. This was something very important to Wittgenstein.

Similarly, Frege and Russell were not satisfied by focusing only on *surface* forms. Russell did not accept the view that the grammar of everyday use of language is the ultimate standard. Rather, he searched for a different underlying logical structure. It is in this spirit that Wittgenstein's first step towards a work in philosophy, the *Notes on Logic*, were undertaken together with Russell. But in 1937 Wittgenstein acknowledged Sraffa for having made him see that not all meaningful uses of language can be described in logical notation or formal grammar (Ms-157b,5v). The fact that Sraffa is last on the list of the ten figures makes chronological sense. In 1930–1 Wittgenstein had started to play with the idea that rules of language are, in contrast to alleged norms rooted in logical form, mere descriptions of actual language use. Thanks to his discussions with Sraffa, Wittgenstein recognised that also this idea was flawed.[108] It has been argued that Wittgenstein's philosophical references to Sraffa 'are almost always in connexion with the relation between a grammatical rule and an empirical proposition'.[109]

Finally, Wittgenstein's language-game method can also be seen as closely related to Sraffa's influence. From the beginning this method came with a clear recommendation, namely: to stick as much as possible with *simple* language-games (BBB 17). To study language in its simplest forms and to compare philosophical language with the simplest forms of everyday language – whether real or fictional, one's own or an exotic people's everyday language – occupied a central role in this method. The first language-game that occurs in the *Investigations*, the shopping example from §1, was in December 1933 (Ms-115,79–80) brought in as a 'use of language' intended to bring back the philosophically complex concept of

---

[104] See also Haller 1988: 119.   [105] Spengler 1927: 50.
[106] Spengler 1927: 5 (1920: 5: 'Laune').   [107] Spengler 1927: ch. III.
[108] See Engelmann 2013: 117–8 and Brusotti 2016: 50–1.   [109] Munz 2016: 72.

meaning to simple, everyday uses of language. The earliest version of the *Investigations*' second language-game, the builders' language from July 1931 (Ms-111,16–7), was designed to help bring back the general philosophical concept of names and naming to *simple* and unproblematic scenarios of language use such as in constructing a building. This language consists of nothing but four words for four building blocks – cube, column, slab and beam. While the philosophical concept of names and naming, as the foundation and essence ('Fundament und Um-und-Auf', Ms-111,15) of language, is highly problematic, the builders' language-game and its terming as 'complete primitive language' are in §2 presented as unproblematic. It has been widely pointed out that even this very simple builders' language is all but unproblematic, in part precisely because of its primitiveness.[110] In the *Investigations*, it is brought in as a means to clarify the philosophical presuppositions behind Augustine's description of language, but it was meant more as an illustration of the thinking in the *Tractatus*. The principle of sticking to simple or primitive language-games remains valid also where the method turns from using language-games as 'objects of comparison' (§122) to attending to *examples* of the concept to be clarified. For example, in order to clarify the concept of rule-following, Wittgenstein refers in the *Investigations* to the simplest cases of rule-following and studies concrete examples of following a signpost, of obeying an order, of moving according to the instructions from a table, of reading or of continuing a mathematical series.

However, Wittgenstein had also learned from Sraffa that looking *merely* at language and action, that is the language-game, is not sufficient for philosophical clarification. Language-games always come embedded in a life and are thus related to the role the word plays in this life (see BBB 93, 94, 103). The language-game method is therefore to be paired with attention to the 'form of life' ('Lebensform'; see §19, §23, §25, §241, §415) which language and action are constituted by. A brief circumscription of this method is given in §19: 'And to imagine a language means to imagine a form of life'. Sraffa has been credited for having given Wittgenstein, in addition to the '"anthropological" way of looking at philosophical problems',[111] the related ethnological method which is highly prominent not only in the *Brown Book* but also in much later writings where Wittgenstein asks us to 'imagine a tribe ...'. While, going back to Ramsey, the anthropological turn saw Wittgenstein adequately bringing into philosophy the constitutive role of the human as such, the ethnological perspective brings in human and cultural *diversity* as they are present in the works of Spengler[112] and Frazer but also Malinowski, who early had endorsed an

---

[110] See for example 'Wittgenstein's Builders' in Rhees 1970.   [111] Monk 1990: 261.
[112] See Engelmann 2013: 296 and 2016: 134–5.

ethnological approach to language and meaning.[113] According to Rhees, Wittgenstein 'used to say that what we might call "the anthropological method" had proved particularly fruitful in philosophy: that is, imagining "a tribe among whom it is carried on in this way: ...".'[114] Sraffa himself uses anthropological and ethnological methods when he begins his *Production of Commodities* by imagining a society with simplest possible economics: 'Let us consider an extremely simple society which produces just enough to maintain itself...'.[115] 'Ethnological' method helps us take 'our position far outside, in order to see the things more *objectively*' (CV 37/45).

§2 contains both a language-game and a move in the spirit of ethnological method. It is the turn from *A is a too simple and therefore false description of B*, to *A is a correct description of a simpler B; namely, the primitive language-game B'*. While this figure of thought or thought movement is foreshadowed by TLP 5.156 '(A proposition ...)', it is also possible that it is closely connected with an argument that Wittgenstein originally voiced against Plato. The early version of Wittgenstein's critique of Augustine's description of the learning of language is framed by citations from *Theaetetus* discussions on whether representing something wrongly amounts to representing *nothing* (Ms-111,14–20; 1931). With his chiasmus-like move, Wittgenstein makes it clear that a false representation of X can still be a correct representation of X'. The correctly represented object X' is then made into a language-game that functions as an object of comparison. Furthermore, for the language-game a form of life is then imagined where it is at home. Comparing the builders' language and its larger setting as the 'whole language of a tribe' (§6) to ours helps us better understand *our* language and its role in *our* life. Wittgenstein's language-game method could thus be anchored in a move that originally opposed Plato. Plato himself makes the move of §2, for example when he in *Laches* lets Socrates point out that Laches' answer to the question 'What is courage?' was not correct for courage in general (X), but only with regard to a certain form of courage (X').

The method of developing a small, primitive language-game into a series of increasingly complex language-games, as it characterises the *Brown Book*, can also be associated with Sraffa – even though 'the use that Wittgenstein makes of the idea of primitive cultures and growing complexity is certainly quite different from Sraffa's'.[116] Sraffa had, in his book, expanded the initial simple economic model with more and more complexities. Furthermore, we can assume that it was not only Sraffa's 'criticism' (Preface) but also Wittgenstein's experience of Sraffa's Italian expressiveness embodied in rich body language that must have

---

[113] Malinowski 1923; see also Brusotti 2018.   [114] Rhees 1970: 101.   [115] Sraffa 1960: 3.
[116] Engelmann 2013: 295; see also Andrews 1996: 770–2.

impressed him. The Neapolitan gesture made it obvious to Wittgenstein that there *is* no meaning to a sign without the larger culture and form of life to which it belongs: 'it's an ethnological fact – it's something to do with the way we live' (LFM 249). Wittgenstein's remark that a language-game is one only in the context of a whole culture (LA 8) must surely be related to Sraffa – but it could also again be related to Loos.[117]

2.5 Frege's Transformations and Elucidations

Wittgenstein might well have learned to return philosophical thought and language to everyday practices and contexts from Sraffa. But if we concentrate on methods of *Zurückführung* as such, Frege is the key figure. Frege sought to transform – all without gaps – logical laws to other logical laws, functions to other functions, numbers to properties of concepts and finally, arithmetic to logic (in Wittgenstein's words: 'Zurückführung der Arithmetik auf symbolische Logik', Ms-122,12v-13r; 1939). One function of such transformation is to make the superfluous disappear. Another is to demystify and eliminate what is problematic in a certain concept. As a result, for example, 'numbers of every kind, whether negative, fractional, irrational or complex, are revealed as no more mysterious than the positive whole numbers, which in turn are no more real or more actual or more palpable than they'.[118] Mystifying concepts can make us feel uneasy – their transformation into concepts that are not problematic reassures us and makes us feel at home. One of Wittgenstein's pictures for the perturbed and panicking philosopher is the philosopher (the solipsist) going wild and fluttering their wings in the fly-bottle (LPE 258, Ms-149,34r-34v; 1935–6). The philosopher troubled by their problem resembles the stressed bird fluttering from one wall to another. First of all, the philosopher is 'zur Ruhe zu bringen' (LPE 258): they are to get from panic to peace. This does not necessarily mean that they should be brought completely to a stop, but just put back in control so that 'calm progress' ('ruhiges Fortschreiten', Ts-213,431r) becomes possible.

Frege became an inspiration for Wittgenstein also on another level. When forming philosophical books for the reader, Wittgenstein found a special use for Frege's thought on the role elucidations ('Erläuterungen') and hints ('Winke') have in communicating with the reader.[119] The translation of 'erläutern' as 'elucidate' seems to have been suggested by Wittgenstein himself.[120] Elucidations are there for the *reader* – the author does not need them for themselves.[121] But since elucidations only belong to the propaedeutics of science,

---

[117] Westergaard 1995: 288. [118] Frege 1974: §109. [119] See Bengtsson 2018.
[120] See CCO 1973: 51, 54 as well as LPA 2016: RamseyTranslation,83r_f and OgdenQuestionnaire,8r_f.
[121] Frege 1906: 301 (1984: 301).

they should not be taken as expressing final statements of science or philosophy. Rather, after they have done their job, they should be discarded by the reader. The 'discard me afterwards' aspect of elucidation becomes central for Wittgenstein's work on forming his book. He utilises this aspect of elucidation when he terms his sentences 'elucidatory' in TLP 6.54 and thereby signals to the reader that all theses and doctrines that have entered the book's scaffolding must eventually be dropped: 'He must so to speak throw away the ladder, after he has climbed up on it.' It has been argued that this move bears a resemblance to Kierkegaard's/ Climacus' strategy in the *Concluding Unscientific Postscript*.[122] In a strict sense, according to Frege, elucidations cannot be *understood*. But they can help us understand *the author*. This sense of 'elucidation' is invoked when Wittgenstein in TLP 6.54 'does not ask that his propositions be understood, but that *he* be'.[123]

2.6 Spengler and Schopenhauer's Family Resemblances

We saw that Frege was a central figure for Wittgenstein when forming at least two of his books. In the *Tractatus*, Wittgenstein sought to put Frege's ideal of gapless sequence and procedure to work in the form of a ladder. The *Tractatus* ladder should not lack any rungs. The main rungs of the ladder, the cardinal propositions, were worded so that they pointed backwards to the previous cardinal proposition and forwards to the next. This composition made a tight chain out of the propositions. The same ideal form of gapless sequence was pursued in the *Brown Book* where not only Frege but also Goethe and Spengler were at work. Goethe and Spengler's morphological method advocated arrangement of the cardinal elements 'as clearly indicated steps of a stepladder free of gaps'.[124] The cardinal elements of the *Brown Book* were its language-games. In the transition from the *Brown Book* to the *Investigations*, Wittgenstein gave up gapless sequencing and the stepladder.

But it is likely that Spengler was an important influence also on the forming of the *Investigations*. Spengler has the penultimate position on Wittgenstein's list of influences and he was one of the original four figures on the list. He surely played a role in Wittgenstein's adoption of the idea of family resemblance that is central to later Wittgenstein's philosophy of language (§§66–71). Whether Wittgenstein's idea of family resemblance actually has its 'origin in Spengler's notion of the *Ursymbol* (archetype)'[125] or rather arises 'out of a critique formulated *against* Spengler',[126] is unclear. Similarly, it may be argued that also Wittgenstein's idea of perspicuous representation from the

---

[122] Conant 1997. [123] Diamond 1991: 19. [124] Schulte 1992: 81–2.
[125] von Wright: 1982: 213. [126] Engelmann 2013: 295 (my italics).

beginning was formed *in opposition to*, rather than *in accordance with*, Spengler's idea of morphological method.[127] It is however settled that Wittgenstein explicitly referred to Spengler in May 1932 when he mentioned 'people', 'king' and 'religion' as examples of family resemblance concepts (PG II §13, Ms-113,102v). The earliest explicit reference by Wittgenstein to 'Familienähnlichkeit' in Spengler can be found in Ms-111,119–20 of 19.8.1931 (see BT 204). Spengler used the term for similarity in art history style phases.[128] He had also recurrently figured in the versions of §122, the remark that endorses perspicuous representation as a method of philosophy, up to 1937. Since the transition from the *Brown Book* to the *Investigations* can be seen as a transition from aspiring at linear and gapless perspicuous representation to quite a *different* mode of perspicuous representation, namely a form along the principles of criss-crossing and intertwining family resemblances, (opposition to) Spengler could then be seen to have played a role also in this development. Ironically, in the proto-version of §122 Wittgenstein *criticised* Spengler for having misused the idea of family resemblances when creating out of it 'ideal types' or 'archetypes'.

While the origins of family resemblance are commonly traced back to Spengler, one could trace them back yet further. However, Wittgenstein's idea of family resemblance and the related special method for forming the *Investigations* may originate earlier than 1930, the year that he read Spengler (MT 25; 6.5.1930). Once we look for sources outside Spengler, several other candidates appear.[129] They include Stewart, Galton, James, Nicod, Nietzsche and Weininger. Recall that Weininger aimed at bringing the dichotomy between male and female, and thus the apparent unity of each of the two concepts, back to the actual, existing motley of *intermediate forms*. When Wittgenstein introduces the idea of family resemblance in the *Investigations*, his wording bears a striking similarity to Weininger's remark about the 'countless similarities and differences' with which the world confuses our intellect.[130] Moreover, Weininger emphasised that it is only in our concepts that sharp boundaries are drawn while the world itself is characterised by 'continuous transitions'.[131] One concept which Weininger finds extremely difficult, if not impossible, to define is 'Jewishness'; in his description of the concept Weininger gives a fine example of attending to family resemblance that might have inspired Wittgenstein. Weininger uses the expression 'Familienähnlichkeit' itself only once, citing it from Jean Paul.[132]

---

[127] Engelmann 2016: 148–53. [128] Spengler 1920: 278 (1927: 202).
[129] See also Baker and Hacker 2005a: 207–9.
[130] Weininger 1904: 3: 'zahllose Ähnlichkeiten und Unterschiede'.
[131] Weininger 1904: 5: 'stetige Übergänge'; 10 *et passim*: 'unzählige Zwischenformen'.
[132] See Weininger 1904: 526, 602.

Style, Method and Philosophy in Wittgenstein

Perhaps family resemblance can be traced back even to Wittgenstein's 'earliest philosophical reading', before 1906.[133] For it was at this time that Wittgenstein read *Schopenhauer*, who uses the expression when discussing the infinite variability of both the organic and the inorganic world. 'Family resemblance' provides, according to Schopenhauer, the unity in the variation.[134] Thus, Wittgenstein quite possibly got the idea and composition principle of family resemblance from Schopenhauer in the first place. There is much to suggest that Wittgenstein, when forming the *Tractatus*, partly used Schopenhauer's *Will and Representation* as a template.[135] This included the ladder simile which was already part of Schopenhauer's opus.[136] It is not unlikely that Schopenhauer was important for the forming of the *Investigations*, too. There are remarks from the autumn of 1933 that lend support to this idea of a Schopenhauerian influence on the specific way of composing the *Investigations*: in the *Yellow Book*, Wittgenstein approvingly cites Schopenhauer's view that a philosophical book is to be 'an organism' (YB §1). In the *Pink Book*, he complements Schopenhauer's view that 'one could not understand one bit without knowing the whole'; the organic intertwining and criss-cross structure of grammar makes it necessary that the philosopher goes 'over and over again the same connections': 'This is where Schopenhauer's repetition comes in' (DPS 103–4).[137] Repetition becomes unavoidable when one works and writes along the lines of family resemblances. The same threads, while not running through all elements treated, and the same nodes while not being crosspoints for all threads, will turn up again and again. Repetition and 'traversing zig-zag paths'[138] was, therefore, not only a necessary constituent in Wittgenstein's 'way of philosophizing' (CV 1/3) but also for the form of his philosophical *works*. If one wants to do perspicuous representation in the form of linear and gapless sequence, repetition will *have* to come in so often that it may become annoying. For the gapless linear series of the *Brown Book*, repetition thus posed a challenge rather than a possibility. But as soon as the perspicuous representation was freed from the idol of gapless linear sequence, repetition could become a positive element also for the book that Wittgenstein wanted to compose for the reader from his own philosophising.

---

[133] McGuinness 1988: 39; see also Anscombe in Erbacher et al. 2019: 231.
[134] Schopenhauer 1873: vol. I, book 2, §§17, §27, §28; vol. II, ch. 31.
[135] See Janik 1985: 26–47. [136] Schopenhauer 1873: vol. II, ch. 7.
[137] See Schopenhauer 1873: Vorrede and vol. II, ch. 31. See also Neumer 2000: 246. For the *Pink Book* see DPS ch. 3.
[138] Anscombe 1969: 375.

2.7 Development of Philosophy and Authorship in Wittgenstein

If Wittgenstein had the concept of family resemblance with him at least since 1930, or since his reading of Weininger – if not since his first reading of Schopenhauer – how shall we explain that this device was not put to work for the composition of his book before late 1936? Two things are to be considered here: first, Wittgenstein himself tells us that philosophy does not face *intellectual* challenges only, but also that 'resistance of the *will* must be overcome' (BT 301). The idea and the methods of criss-cross perspicuous representation along principles of family resemblance may well have been available to him earlier, but still Wittgenstein might not have wanted to admit them then into his philosophy. Wittgenstein's philosophical development was at least as much a development of attitude and will as it was of cognition. In the *Pink Book*, Wittgenstein explicitly brings in Schopenhauer when he discusses resistance of the will in philosophy: 'Schopenhauer once said, "If you try to convince someone and get to a certain resistance, you then know you are up against the will, not the understanding"' (DPS 43). Second, when it comes to the specific criss-cross forming of the *Investigations*, we have to recognise that this work is the outcome of hard labour and composition. In other words, the *Investigations* is born of studious editing and composing of remarks written earlier *into* criss-cross form, rather than simply a process of copying remarks that originally were already written in criss-cross form. The creation of the *Investigations* along principles of criss-crossing, rather than gapless, perspicuous representation, was therefore a result of careful and intense effort. As such, it was the achievement of a design given to this specific *work*, rather than being a format characterising all Wittgensteinian writing, including writing from the *Investigations* onwards. Not surprisingly, we can find in the *Nachlass*, also *after* the *Investigations* have taken form as an album, texts produced in a form very different from album form.[139] This chimes in with the fact that the criss-cross album form itself was already largely described in the November 1930 'preface' remarks. Just like family resemblance, the form may have been available to Wittgenstein for a long time. It was just not put to work until 1936. Or it was again put to work in 1936, if one were to count the 'Philosophische Bemerkungen' of Ts-209 from 1930 as Wittgenstein's *first* album.[140]

This way of taking into account 'delayed influences' and 'asynchronicities' in Wittgenstein contrasts with more standard ways of presenting Wittgenstein's philosophical and literary development under a template of successive progress and step-by-step change.[141] One example is the following view: after his return to

---

[139] See Pichler 2007: 140; Pichler 2018: 58 and Trächtler 2021: 22–3. [140] See Pichler 2009.
[141] See Pichler 2018.

Cambridge, Wittgenstein takes up questions and issues that were left unsatisfactorily dealt with in the *Tractatus,* which leads him to his 'phenomenological' philosophy; problems arising from this new philosophy as well as the philosophy of others (such as Russell) bring him to develop the calculus conception of language; the calculus conception is in turn later replaced by the anthropological conception.[142] This analysis follows a 'not yet there, but coming next' scheme. Passages that do not fit into this scheme are attributed to 'Wittgenstein's opponent', whose basic role it is to present the views to be overcome. However, the alternative approach sketched here, abandoning the 'first a, then b' scheme, may well often make more sense. It acknowledges that a and b may both be *simultaneously* present in Wittgenstein's thought, but that it is the weighting and rating which each receives that changes.[143] Another example of the standard 'first a, then b' perspective is the idea that the principal contribution of the ten figures is that each of them brought Wittgenstein 'a step onward'.[144] It seems reasonable to abandon the 'first a, then b' view also on this point.

Seen in this light, it becomes understandable that the calculus and the anthropological conception may *both* already be present on an equal footing in the *Big Typescript,* and that the calculus conception is only *one* of the *Big Typescript*'s lines of argument.[145] As a consequence, it is not so much that the calculus conception is later replaced by the anthropological conception, but rather that its role in certain contexts becomes qualified and restricted, yet it is still active and awaiting new tasks elsewhere. If we adopt this view, the anthropological approach, far from being a deus ex machina that is first found in the *Brown Book* or the *Philosophical Investigations,* can be available to Wittgenstein much earlier, even if he was not yet ready to give it its later role. This fits again well with what Wittgenstein says in the *Big Typescript* itself, namely: that the difficulty of philosophy is 'not the intellectual difficulty of the sciences, but the difficulty of a change of attitude. Resistance of the will must be overcome' (BT 301). Accordingly, both Wittgenstein's philosophical development and the development of the forms of his works are to be regarded, as much as intellectual struggles, struggles of the will.

3 Poetry in Philosophy

3.1 Poetry in Writing Philosophy, Poetry in Forming Philosophical Works

In Section 1.3, in the context of the *Tractatus*' philosophy of language, I presented the following interpretation of Wittgenstein's remark that philosophy should really be done only in the mode of poetry: when philosophy has said

---

[142] Engelmann 2013. [143] See also Stern 2004: 53. [144] McGuinness 1988: 84.
[145] See Pichler 2018.

all it *can* say, what it still wants to say will have to be left to poetry.[146] We are now in a position to amend this interpretation in a twofold way. The *author* of the *Tractatus* would surely agree with both points.

First, it is not enough to bring in poetry only when philosophy is done with its business. Poetry is required already *in* the act of clarification. In fact, Wittgenstein once asked in late 1946 why, when writing philosophy, he feels like he is writing a poem (Ms-133,13r). Writing philosophy includes for Wittgenstein attending to prosody and tone, indeed the 'sonic quality of phrases and sentences', rather than 'the conceptual and abstract language of making meaningful propositions' only.[147] Poetry *in* the act of clarification helps to find the redeeming word ('das erlösende Wort'). The redeeming word is, first and foremost, the phrase that permits us to capture what the philosophical problem consists in, and second, it is also the phrase that permits us to finally dispose of the philosophical problem. Already at the very beginning of the *Investigations* (§1) we find a redeeming word in the first sense. It is the following: 'the words in language name objects – sentences are combinations of such names'. This phrasing nails down a specific philosophical conception of meaning and lays bare its components for treatment. The activity of bringing philosophy's concepts back to everyday language where the words do work can begin only when such a redeeming word is found. Then also 'grammatical unclarity' can be made to disappear (BT 302). In order to find the redeeming word, as well as for the activity of philosophical clarification in general, 'rejecting false arguments' (BT 302) is not enough. Grammatical deviance or mere unclarity is frequently much better countered by poetic thought experiments, pictures, analogies, comparisons, metaphors and similes than by formal argument. Often it is precisely 'a false analogy' (BT 302) that needs to be challenged by the right analogy so that one can find the word 'with which we can express the matter and render it harmless' (BT 302). Not only is argument not enough, not all convincing can or must proceed by arguments either. Moreover, for countering false analogies or views, enlarging our imaginations may be required. Why should widening the imagination only be something that 'is all right for novelists to do, but not all right for philosophers?'[148]

From Ernst (1910) Wittgenstein had learned that the mythology 'laid down in our language' (BT 317), and with it the images according to which we conceive of ourselves and the world can be utterly misleading; this includes images for the mental.[149] Our 'grammatical problems ... are connected with the oldest thought habits, i.e. with the oldest images that are engraved into our language

---

[146] Ms-146,25v and Ms-115,30; see also Ms-146,16v: 'Die Darstellung der Philosophie kann nur gedichtet werden'. All three probably stem from December 1933.
[147] Cf. Perloff 2004: 36–7.   [148] See Diamond 1991: 293–4.   [149] See Trächtler 2021: ch. 2.

itself' (BT 311). In this context, Wittgenstein also mentions Lichtenberg. Philosophy is to clear away false mythologies, rather than building new ones on them (BT 111); philosophy is to *clean* our thinking of false mythologies (Ms-109,210–11; 1930). But Ernst had equally shown that the same mythology also preserves our deepest positive beliefs and conceptual schemes.[150] These are accessible through myths, fairy tales and pictures rather than science and rational discourse. The poetic use of pictorial language and similes is therefore a must for bringing us back to the layer where we can again see the world aright. Finally, poetry may be specifically required where a *last* 'resistance of the will' (BT 301) is to be overcome. When argument already has done its job of clarifying the philosophical concepts and problem, the philosopher may still not want to let go of them. A final powerful poetic picture may then be needed.[151]

Secondly, poetry is also required to give the philosophical book its apt *form*. In Section 1.1, a distinction was made between Wittgenstein's philosophical 'reactions' in writing, on the one hand, and the book formed out of the 'precipitate' (Preface) from the philosophical clarification, on the other. Each attempt that Wittgenstein made to form a book for the reader was an attempt at forming this precipitate so that it could help the reader address and solve their own philosophical problems. At one point in the early 1930s, he played with the idea of offering only single *Bemerkungen* (Ms-154,9v-10r). But, as he puts it in the November 1930 'preface' remarks, an ideal that was considered equally was that the book should provide an organisation, an order, indeed be *culture* assigning each remark to its proper place. The act of forming the book for the reader is consequently regarded by Wittgenstein as an act of *culture*, for 'culture is like a great organisation which assigns to each of its members his place' (CV 6/8). The 'members' in question here are Wittgenstein's *remarks*, and the remarks are to be *organised* such that each remark 'can work in the spirit of the whole, and [its] strength can with a certain justice be measured by [its] success as understood within that whole' (CV 6/9). As long as the remarks are unorganised, they belong to a 'time without culture', where 'forces are fragmented and the strength of the individual is wasted through the overcoming of opposing forces & frictional resistances; it is not manifest in the distance travelled but rather perhaps in the heat generated through the overcoming of frictional resistances' (CV 6/9). According to these early programmatic statements, the forces, which are often opposed or at least fragmented in the act of clarification, shall be joined and channelled together for the reader into one

---

[150] See also Malinowski 1923: 328 about 'grammatical categories'.
[151] See also Klagge 2021: ch. 4.

conducive force in the book. This book would, ideally, offer the reader a way to grasp Wittgenstein's own ways of clarification and provide them with examples they could follow as they undertake their own acts of clarification. As a conscious act of forming, each single attempt at creating the book for the reader was therefore also an act of poetry and culture.[152]

Poetry thus accompanied Wittgenstein's philosophical authorship throughout his life. Rather than offering single *Bemerkungen* or remarks only (a 'bag of raisins', CV 66/76), it was crucial to give the reader a work of culture by weaving the *Bemerkungen* into a holistic form. For the *Tractatus*, this form had been the ladder. The later Wittgenstein, as he himself pointed out in the preface to the *Investigations*, had different ideas about the organisation of his remarks in the book at different times. The most prominent format of the first half of the 1930s was the *Betrachtung* for which Wittgenstein closely cooperated with Waismann. However, in the autumn of 1934 the *Betrachtung* format was superseded by the linear sequence of the *Brown Book*. More than any other book of the 1930s, the *Brown Book* sought to mould the contents into a gapless linear sequence. But two years later, in the late autumn of 1936, Wittgenstein would feel that it had 'cramped' his thinking (ICE: To Moore 20.11.1936). For the subsequent *Investigations*, he would embark on composing a less rigid format for his book, namely: that of the album. Though less rigid, the album does not require any less 'very careful organisation'.[153] With the album, Wittgenstein sought once again to give the single remarks the status and role they both deserved and required, rather than subordinating them to linear sequencing.[154] The place from which the remarks 'can work in the spirit of the whole' (CV 6/9) was not to be the rung of a stepladder.

3.2 The *Investigations* as a *Fragment* of the *Brown Book*

The general sequencing of the *Investigations* will be as a chronologically arranged philosophical autobiography. In addition, it became a principle for composing the *Investigations* that it should point back to the text from which it had directly originated, namely: the *Brown Book*. In preface drafts, Wittgenstein says in the summer of 1938 that his *Investigations* begins 'with the fragment of my last attempt to arrange my philosophical thoughts in an ordered sequence. This fragment has perhaps the advantage of giving comparatively easily an idea of my method. I intend to follow up this fragment with a mass of remarks more or less loosely arranged ...' (Ts-247,2r; translation by Redpath). By the 'last attempt' Wittgenstein means the *Brown Book*, by 'fragment' the first part of the

---

[152] See also Keicher 2000 and Erbacher 2015. [153] Anscombe 1969: 376.
[154] See also Erbacher 2015: 20.

so-called early version of the *Investigations* (Ts-220, corresponding to roughly §§1–188).[155] Wittgenstein told Moore that in the *Brown Book* he had followed the wrong method, but he followed the right method in the *Investigations* (EPB 12–3). In *both* works Wittgenstein had followed the language-game method. However, for the *Brown Book* this method was the *predominant* method. The *Investigations*, in contrast, shows that the language-game method is not sufficient to adequately address all philosophical concepts and problems, or also to adequately address all facets of a philosophical problem, and complements it with a plurality of other methods, including dialogue.[156]

Moreover, in the *Brown Book* the language-game method had been paired with an idea of perspicuous representation as a *linear and gapless series* of language-games. All gaps in the presentation were to be filled with connecting or 'intermediate links' ('Zwischenglieder'; §122). This required great skills in composition. Many of the gaps had to be filled with invented ('erdichtete') language-games. The ideals of *linearity* and *gapless* sequence put strong constraints on the formation and procedure of the book. In everyday life and language, *any* language-game is a conglomerate of a great variety of different activities and components. Even language-game (1) in the *Brown Book*, containing only four nouns, comprises already demonstrative teaching (pointing to an object, directing the attention to it, pronouncing the word for it) and demonstrative learning (learning to 'name' the object), as well as ordering (calling out the word for an object) and obeying an order (bringing the object ordered). Going on to the next language-game, Wittgenstein will, for the sake of linear and gapless sequence, ideally want to continue from at least one of these components, before introducing new ones. The new components introduced in language-game (2) are learning the numerals from one to five by heart, learning to count from one to five and learning how to count objects with these numerals. With language-game (3) Wittgenstein has now the opportunity to introduce yet other functionalities, but only on the premise that it can be related back to either language-game (1) or (2) by a component that it shares with them: it is pointing to an object, pronouncing its name and fetching it, but this time the activities are related to a proper name (which is the new functionality introduced). And so on. Needless to say, this procedure will force Wittgenstein to repeatedly postpone the treatment of functionalities that appear in the new language-game and are not the ones he wishes to focus on at the moment. Simultaneously, he will again and again have to refer back to earlier language-games that offered treatments and discussion of what is entangled with what stands in focus now. The *Brown Book* abounds with

---

[155] For alternative accounts see Keicher 2004; Baker and Hacker 2005b: 1–6 and Rothhaupt 2011.
[156] See also Conant 2011: 640.

examples of both moves. Most importantly, if the continuation from one language-game to the next one seems broken – if there apparently is no property that links the desired new language-game with the previous one(s) – then he needs to *find* or *invent* yet another language-game as a bridge between them, that is a connecting 'intermediate link'.

Clearly, the *Brown Book* method demanded much more systematisation and linearity than was suitable for Wittgenstein's project. The ideal of linear gapless sequence and the compulsive order that came with it turned out to be more of an obstacle than a help. It was a bad idolum in Bacon's sense rather than a positive ideal. Wittgenstein wrote to Moore from Skjolden:

> when I came here [end of August] I began to translate into & rewrite in German the stuff I had dictated to Skinner & Miss Ambrose [the *Brown Book*]. When about a fortnight ago [beginning of November], I read through what I had done so far I found it all, or nearly all, boring & artificial. For having the english version before me had cramped my thinking. I therefore decided to start all over again & not to let my thoughts be guided by anything but themselves. – I found it difficult the first day or two [Ms-152 and Ms-140,39v, beginning of Ms-142] but then it became easy. And so I'm writing now a new version [the *Investigations* proto-version in Ms-142] & I hope I'm not wrong in saying that it's somewhat better than the last. (ICE: To Moore 20.11.1936)

Moreover, as a book that ideally 'contained nothing of philosophy', the *Brown Book* was not suited to bring to light the great number and variety of philosophical problems and issues. On its premises, it was simply not possible to deal successfully with all philosophical language and thought. However, while Wittgenstein became sceptical about the *Brown Book*, it was not the language-game method as a philosophical method that he questioned. This method remained something that is endorsed also in the *Investigations*, but now we find it in a 'fragmented' rather than in the original gapless sequence form, and embedded in an 'album' (Preface). The *Investigations* 'lives', in Cavell's words, 'on the sound of the fragment, the denial of system (while by no means the denial of the systematic)'.[157] Cavell terms the *Investigations*' way of doing perspicuous representation in more non-formal, non-discursive and fragmentary ways as 'aphoristic'. It is aphoristic form that is capable of both granting 'the appeal ... of the metaphysical' *and* of 'leading a word back from its metaphysical capture by the appeal to its everyday use'.[158] It is therefore in

---

[157] Cavell 2004: 32. See also Venturinha 2013 who draws a parallel to the 'fragmentation' of Pascal's *Pensées*.
[158] Cavell 2004: 29.

the *aphoristic* that Cavell finds the unity between the philosophy and style of the *Investigations*.

3.3 The *Investigations* as an *Album*

Choosing the album over, for example, the ladder form does not yet commit the author to a specific *arrangement* as such. The question then arises: what are the principles underlying the specific arrangement of the remarks in the *Investigations*? A clue to answering this question is again found in the preface to the *Investigations*. There Wittgenstein tells us that with his album he wants to 'give the viewer an idea of the landscape' he had been travelling through on his philosophical journeys. The organisation of the *Investigations* album thus follows the format of a philosophical autobiography, telling the reader about parts of the philosophical clarifications Wittgenstein undertook in 'the last sixteen years' (Preface). Let us remember that §1 begins with a quote from another personal and autobiographical book, Augustine's *Confessions*. Since November 1936 Wittgenstein has used Augustine's description of how language is learned for the specific task of introducing the *Tractatus* picture of language to be critiqued. Now Augustine is also given the role of introducing a philosophical book of a confessional, biographical nature.[159] The unity of the *Investigations*' style and philosophy is therefore also given in its confessional and autobiographical form: 'Le style c'est l'homme même' (CV 78/89). For Cavell, the 'claim for the aphoristic, say for its mode of expressiveness, rests upon experience, the claim's own perspicuousness depends upon attracting to itself sufficient pertinent experience'.[160] With the album of the *Investigations*, Wittgenstein then offers, as material and as proof, examples from the rich palette of his own philosophical experiences that he had on his 'long and meandering journeys' (Preface).

If one considers the *Investigations* as also belonging to the genre of philosophical autobiography, what then are the principles underlying the specific arrangement of its records? As we have noted, the contents of an album can be arranged according to a number of different parameters. Wittgenstein could have organised his records of philosophical clarification in terms of, for example, philosophical landscapes he travelled (meaning, philosophy, logic, mind etc.), his discussion partners (the author of the *Tractatus*, Frege, Russell, James etc.), type of means and methods used in philosophical clarification (language-game, deductive or other formal argument, reductio ad absurdum, thought experiment, analogy,

---

[159] For a discussion of the roles biography and autobiography played for Wittgenstein, see Immler 2011.
[160] Cavell 2004: 29.

dialogue etc.), chronology of philosophical journey (first the contents stemming from 1929, then those from 1930 etc.) and so on.

I think that the arrangement of the *Investigations* album is basically a *chronological* one. §§1–189 go back mainly to 1931–7, §§190–326 to 1944–5, §§316–693 to both the 1930s and to 1940–5.[161] Anscombe and Rhees thought in the 1953 edition of the *Investigations* that Wittgenstein 'would have suppressed a good deal of what is in the last thirty pages or so of Part I, and worked what is in Part II, with further material, into its place' (PI 1953: Editor's note).[162] As a consequence, parts at the end of (Part I of) the *Investigations* would then have been replaced with remarks written 1945–9. Von Wright thought that, in 1945, Wittgenstein possibly wanted to continue §§1–188 with 'a new version of the second half of the early version of the *Investigations,* with additions from his many writings on those topics [philosophy of logic and mathematics] during the period 1937–44'.[163] This fits with McGuinness' belief that 'the title "Philosophical Investigations" was always meant to cover the mathematical material as well'.[164] If these conjectures are true, then, if Wittgenstein had the strength and time to carry out his plans, he would have wanted to assemble in the *Investigations* chronologically arranged records from about *twenty* years, 1929–49.

The book would begin with the mentioned 'fragment' (roughly §§1–188) giving 'an idea of my method'. Central elements of the method introduced comprise the language-game method (including 'the method of §2'; §48), attention to form of life, perspicuous representation and awareness and utilisation of family resemblances. Subjects discussed include 'the concepts of "meaning", "understanding", "proposition", "logic"' (Ts-247,1r) – in the phrasing of the *Investigations* preface, 'the concepts of meaning, of understanding, of a proposition and sentence, of logic'. One can hold that Wittgenstein's new outlook on the concepts of meaning and on the nature of exactness and logic also makes part of his method and therefore is rightly endorsed already in the fragment.

The fragment was to be followed by 'a mass of remarks more or less loosely arranged', where the method is applied in depth to, among others, philosophical conceptions of rule and rule-following, privacy, the mental, and, so the plan, also philosophy of mathematics: 'the foundations of mathematics, sensedata, the conflict between realism and idealism, and others' (Ts-247,1r) – in the phrasing

---

[161] See Maury 1994. [162] Cf. von Wright 1992.
[163] von Wright 1982: 132. For further discussion of both the genesis of the *Investigations* and its text as ultimately intended by Wittgenstein, see Stern 1996: 448–9, McGuinness 2002b: 283–6, PI 2009 xviii-xxiii and Rothhaupt 2015.
[164] McGuinness 2002b: 286.

of the *Investigations* preface 'the foundations of mathematics, states of consciousness, and other things'. Already the fragment had given samples of how to *apply* the method, the most extensive being the discussion of reading (roughly §§156–78).

Albums assemble what already exists in its own right *before* the album. The PI album collects 'the precipitate of philosophical investigations which have occupied me for the last sixteen years'. (Preface). Even the *Tractatus* didn't claim to present any new thoughts. Earlier, Hertz had claimed nothing more than a new *arrangement*, an alternative ordering of the principles of mechanics. It was in the *arrangement* of the subject – which he called its logical or philosophical aspect – that Hertz saw the book's value.[165] Philosophy does not teach new facts, Wittgenstein says: 'I shall only tell you trivial things – what you all know.' What philosophy does is bring those trivialities into *synopsis*: 'What's difficult is synopsis – to see them together' (LC 5:13, see also 5.29). What makes an album therefore unique and original is the selection and the synopsis, the arrangement of the items that it brings together. But this removes the original settings of these items. Not surprisingly then, in the *Investigations,* the records of Wittgenstein's philosophical clarifications are stripped of their original contexts. First, the remarks are separated from their original discourses of clarification, including argumentative discourse, and arranged differently. Second, they are additionally 'often cut down, in order to give the viewer an idea of the landscape' (Preface). As a consequence, the original threads of thought and reasoning are no longer available as such in the *Investigations*. This includes the specific discursive moves, logical inferences, suggestions and objections, the complete contexts of argument in which the remarks occurred – in short, the movements of thought ('Gedankenbewegungen') and full dynamics and contents that were at work in the original clarification processes. But we find them in the *Nachlass*. Thus, the album label is also to be taken as an invitation to visit the *Nachlass*.

3.4 The *Investigations* as a *Polyphonic* Dialogue

The turn from the *Brown Book* to the *Investigations* involved a change in the implementation of the *morphological* method that Wittgenstein had adopted from Goethe and Spengler. Following Goethe's original conception, the *Brown Book* aspired to practise morphology in a strictly linear and gapless form.[166] In contrast to it, in the *Investigations* perspicuous representation is composed along principles that permit gaps and leaps and criss-crossings. This is only 'natural', for the field of the investigation – the grammar of language and

---

[165] Hertz 1894: xxvii. [166] Schulte 1990: 11–42.

thought – is itself characterised by a criss-cross structure, and is thus 'a complicated network of similarities overlapping and criss-crossing' (Preface; §66). Wittgenstein now wants to offer a way of exploring grammar in the criss-cross ways it is structured and the ways it is at work from the very beginning. He abandons the attempt to line up in a gapless linear sequence the multiple and multiplying reciprocal family resemblance relations in language. The idea that family resemblance itself may ask for representation in *gapless* structure is in the *Investigations* met with mocking disapproval (§67: 'the continuous [*lückenlose*] overlapping of those fibres'). Philosophy is done best in criss-cross rather than (jigsaw) 'puzzle'[167] form, he thinks now, because it is 'the very nature' of grammar and the philosophical investigation itself which 'compels us to travel criss-cross in every direction over a wide field of thought'. This form will not only permit the gap but will also deliberately introduce it. Any aspiration towards gapless and linear composition will no longer be conceived as 'natural', neither in terms of Wittgenstein as an author nor in terms of the nature of philosophical investigation. This again presents a strong contrast to the *Tractatus*: 'What the *Tractatus* has, and the *Investigations* lacks in this matter of order, is completeness of treatment of each matter before moving on to the next. The *Investigations* does not finish with a topic; it zigzags back to old themes in the context of new subject matter'.[168]

The *Investigations* is receptive to using the full palette of stylistic devices available.[169] This includes humour and jokes since 'nonsense might be called unconscious humour and jokes the conscious form of nonsense'.[170] Anscombe offered one of the earliest descriptions of its style and compared the work to 'a musical composition'.[171] The most striking feature is its specific dialogical and discussion style to which attention has been drawn many times.[172] But while the prevailing response has been to read the *Investigations* as presenting dialogues between an opponent or interlocutor (endorsing philosophical views to be overcome) and the proponent (usually taken to represent Wittgenstein, arguing against these views), this reading does not do justice to the *Investigations*. An alternative is to attribute *both* voices to Wittgenstein – 'the voice of temptation' and 'the voice of correctness' or of 'the everyday'.[173] Another alternative is to distinguish between *three* voices: the interlocutor voice; a non-Pyrrhonian narrator voice; and a Pyrrhonian and therapeutic *commentator* voice. Again, the interlocutor voice is to be overcome, but the narrator voice, proposing philosophical views and argument, is *itself* to be commented upon and balanced by the third voice. In fact, the achievement of the *Investigations* consists in

---

[167] Ortner 2000; see Pichler 2013b.   [168] Anscombe 1969: 375.
[169] See Pichler 2004: ch.6.1.   [170] McGuinness 2006b: 357.   [171] Erbacher et al. 2019: 239.
[172] For example, Cavell 1966, Stern 1996 and Perloff 2011.   [173] Cavell 1966.

keeping the two voices in balance and complementary by means of the third voice, while the tensions between them remain unresolved. In the *Investigations*, the correcting voice of returning philosophy to everyday language is then commented upon and itself overcome; the book upholds critical *engagement* with both 'the voice of temptation' *and* 'the voice of correctness'.[174] Also its motto can be placed in this context and regarded as already in Nestroy's play being spoken by a character comparable to the *Investigations*' commentator voice.[175]

However, even a book that has providing clarifications as its only task cannot eventually avoid putting forward at least some philosophical views. The *Investigations* endorses views about language and grammar, family resemblance and the inseparable bond between language and action. The *Investigations* also advocates a specific view of philosophy, including the view that philosophy's language is properly at home *in functional* everyday language. Ultimately, philosophy can only promote views that 'everyone would agree to': theses in philosophy can ultimately only be platitudes, trivialities (§128, LC 5:13 and 5:29). Also the *Tractatus* could not do without positive views and advocated, for example, the context principle and the sign–symbol distinction (TLP 3.3, 3.32 a.o.). The author of the *Investigations*, like the author of the *Tractatus*, is aware of these scaffoldings. The point is to share with the reader the experience that it is impossible to do philosophical clarification without *any* such scaffoldings, and that to become clear not only about one's positive views but also about the scaffoldings entering one's clarification is an achievement worth striving for. Polyphonic method is capable of adequately acknowledging and bringing in one's own and others' scaffolding.[176] For this goal, a variety of voices is at work in the *Investigations* although not necessarily all of them in each remark and with the same role in all contexts and on each topic. Each voice is legitimate in the project of achieving a better understanding of one's own philosophy and, ideally, also its clarification. Thus we come to realise that eventually the author's voice is not imposed on the reader but is something that each reader has to work out in their own way. To the extent that the scaffoldings themselves turn out to be contestable *philosophical* scaffoldings, the project will be never-ending. The *polyphonic* composition of the *Investigations* therefore offers a treatment of philosophical problems that acknowledges their complexities, open-endedness and personal aspects, much

---

[174] Stern 2004: 5, 21–22, 34–40 and Stern 2017: 48–53.
[175] Stern 2004: 71. Pichler 2004: 162–5 and Stern 2004: 46–55 offer further discussion on the *Investigations*' Pyrrhonism.
[176] 'Polyphonic' is used here as introduced by M. Bakhtin for describing Dostoevsky's poetics (Bakhtin 1984).

more than the mostly single voice omniscient narration and, where dialogical, rather in two-voices-only styled dialogue of the *Blue* and *Brown Book*s. At the same time, it must be said that the Ms-115 German revision of the *Brown Book* (EPB 172-91; cf. BBB 119-25) already included polyphonic portions in the mentioned discussion of reading.[177] This shows once more the complexities of assessing development in Wittgenstein, proving wrong any oversimple perspective of progress along an exclusive 'first a, then b' scheme.

Bringing philosophical language and concepts back to where they are doing work is not as easy as the *Brown Book* had suggested, and the facts they should be brought back to, including the grammatical facts, are significantly more convoluted than the *Brown Book* was able to accommodate.[178] Even if the vision of the goal for the *Investigations* – complete clarity (§133) – might have remained intact, the assessment of how the goal is to be achieved, and to what extent it *can* be achieved, had to be reassessed. The potential and readiness to being tempted into philosophical deviation from grammar is endless. Therefore, the same points had to be 'approached afresh from different directions, and new sketches made' (Preface). *Permanent* clarification of philosophical problems and concepts, in which both the early Wittgenstein and the Wittgenstein of the 1930s up to the late autumn of 1936 had optimistically believed, may not in the end be achievable.[179] Even if philosophical problems are conceptual problems, Wittgenstein tells us now that they cannot be dissolved case by case, piecemeal or by '(finite) horizontal strips'-philosophy ('Querstreifenphilosophie', BT 316).[180] Piecemeal philosophy turns out to be still compatible with a view that Wittgenstein had opposed already in the 1930 'preface' drafts and associated with Western civilisation, namely: the view that philosophical insight can be built in an accumulative way by adding piece to piece like in a jigsaw puzzle. In this view, the individual nodes of this knowledge stand in more or less stable relations to each other so that a fixed coherent whole can be constructed out of them with linearity and progress as structuring principles. In contrast to this view, Wittgenstein's own project, as it materialises in the *Investigations*, is that of philosophy as a continuous clarifying activity that iteratively returns to the same or similar challenges. This requires us to revisit problems that we dealt with previously so that no node remains untouched and can be considered as stable. Re-addressing one node of philosophical insight may have an effect on the place, role and nature of another node, and as a result new conceptual challenges and confusions may arise.

---

[177] For examples of polyphonic readings of the *Investigations*, see Pichler 2004: ch. 5.1 (§§156–178) and Stern 2017: 50–3 (§§256–258 and §372).
[178] See Pichler 2004: chs. 4.2–6.   [179] See also Klagge 2021.
[180] See also Stern 2004: 52–3.

Philosophical problems are thus complexly entangled and developing, and a philosophical work should help the reader to recognise and give voice to their *own* entanglements and developments. Also the notion of family resemblance that is central to the *Investigations* emphasises the criss-cross entanglements and 'overlapping of many fibres' ('einander übergreifen', §67) in our thought, language and life.[181]

Bringing philosophical language and concepts back to everyday language becomes therefore for the Wittgenstein of the *Investigations* a less critical task than facilitating self-insight and self-understanding – seeing oneself aright – in the first place.[182] As such it is highly suitable to provide the 'mirror' that Wittgenstein wanted his philosophical work to be since the early 1930s (CV 18/25). Clarity is now as much about making the philosophical problem in its intrinsic nature clear to ourselves as about gaining an overview of grammar. It is about making clear to ourselves our philosophical nature and situation as a 'modern self ... so estranged from itself and lost to reality'.[183] As there is no limit to the grammatical and voluntative aspects a philosophical problem can take on, there is also no limit to the number and kinds of philosophical voices to be included in the philosophical conversation. Among the many voices the *Investigations* offers, the reader is to find their own voice, as well as another voice to confront themselves with and talk to. The *Investigations*' polyphonic style and '*orchestration* of voice'[184] are therefore in full rapport with Wittgenstein's early statement from 1930 that the only way to acquire the skill required for philosophy is *to discuss* (LC 5:2). Philosophy is no longer 'a matter of invoking a canonical system of rules', but a 'critical dialogue':[185] 'In philosophizing we may not *terminate* [*abschneiden*] a disease of thought. It must run its natural course, and slow cure is all important' (Z §382).

The *Investigations* says: 'Say what you please, so long as it does not prevent you from seeing how things are. (And when you see that, there will be some things that you won't say.)' (§79). This important remark seems to be a late addition to the discussion of the use of the word 'Moses', and to have been written specifically for the *Investigations* proto-version only in the late autumn of 1936 or early spring of 1937 (see Ms-142,68). The *Investigations* can therefore be seen to no longer endorse 'What *we* do is to bring words back from their metaphysical to their everyday use' (§116) as a statement of authoritative and binding method, but only as an expression of a position held earlier

---
[181] See Pichler 2016 and Pichler 2018.
[182] Pichler 2004, Wallgren 2006: ch. 7, Stern 2004: 30, Pichler 2016.   [183] Cavell 2004: 25.
[184] Floyd 2016: 55.
[185] Glock 1996: 261; Glock draws this contrast between the later Wittgenstein and the *Tractatus*, but it should also be drawn between the *Investigations* and the *Blue* and *Brown Books*.

and partaking in the conversation, thus being made explicit and itself becoming 'something for philosophical *treatment*' (§254). But the *Investigations* is, as part of its 'everyday aesthetics of itself', still speaking *in the words and tone* of everyday language, and therefore the reader needs 'no more than the common mastery of a language'.[186]

It is also possible to read the first chapter of the much earlier *Big Typescript* as already staging a polyphonic dialectic, specifically between the calculus and the anthropological conception. And it is also possible to read the *Tractatus* as wanting to provide self-understanding rather than logical or metaphysical insights – as teaching 'that it is only through some confusion one is in about what one is doing that one could take oneself to be putting forward philosophical doctrines or theses at all'.[187] The German word 'erläutern' (TLP 6.54) can be seen to carry with it the notion of cleansing ('läutern'): through elucidations the reader shall be cleansed ('geläutert') of philosophical waste. This shows again that a strongly successive and step-by-step view of Wittgenstein's development of philosophical contents and forms is questionable. Reading the *Big Typescript* or the *Investigations* in polyphonic mode naturally evokes the question of how one attributes a specific remark to a specific voice. Clues are often provided by the text genesis of the remark, for example, by the fact that in its earliest version the remark is embedded in a linear discourse arguing for one of the competing positions.[188]

We see that the album of the *Investigations* is something very different from a mere collection of earlier remarks. The album label does not imply a lack of structure. In fact, it points to a very *specific* structure. It is no mere 'bag' of remarks but a composition that is polyphonically designed. To produce this composition, the remarks to be included 'had to be arranged and often cut down' (Preface). The composition of the polyphonic *Investigations* required from Wittgenstein precisely *composition*, a demanding editorial process on paper. Without editing and composition, no album can emerge. This helps us understand why much of the *Nachlass* writing *post Investigations* is *not* in the album form but again rather '*Bemerkungen* only'; or why, in a further contrast, they take the form of linear discourse. Even though the album form was used in the *Investigations*, it was not a form that could simply be continued in subsequent first writing without further labour and ado. The album form is dependent on laborious editing and composing together of the texts as written. It is not first writing, but rather the outcome of a repeated process of compositional *re*-writing and *re*-arranging. Here we also see why polyphonic structure could not enter Wittgenstein's lecturing. It is true that Wittgenstein's lectures deviated

---

[186] Cavell 2004: 24.　[187] Diamond 1991: 179.　[188] See Pichler 2018.

from some of the prevailing norms of his times and that he discussed and developed new ideas in his lectures. Moreover, he did not use them for one-way communication only. But Wittgenstein could nevertheless not lecture polyphonically, with a 'dialectic between different voices' (LC xlii). Polyphony could not be accomplished spontaneously in the lecturing setting, but required sustained editing and composition. Wittgenstein's lecturing can be compared to his first writing; it was ongoing philosophical clarifications and reactions, rather than precipitates and compositions out of these first reactions.[189]

3.5 The *Investigations* as an Organic Book

Both the *Yellow Book* and the *Pink Book* from 1933–4 had begun with a programmatic declaration that philosophy is to give a perspicuous representation of the (depth) grammar of language. This allows one to achieve an overview or synoptic view of language. But the structure of this grammar is like a 'labyrinth' (§203). Therefore, according to Wittgenstein, Schopenhauer was right in saying that 'one could not understand one bit without knowing the whole' (DPS 103–4), and that one will have to read his book twice.[190] Due to the labyrinthine structure of grammar one cannot make a fully serviceable 'map' of its 'geography' before one has travelled all the 'roads' and acquainted oneself with all the 'connections between the roads' of the entire 'country'. One must 'go over and over again the same connections' (DPS 104). The *Investigations* therefore resonates with a point already made in the November 1930 'preface' comments. There Wittgenstein says that he wants to offer 'the whole thing' (CV 7/9) with each single sentence. It is difficult to show 'the whole thing' with one single sentence or remark. Therefore the book will have to provide the overview by showing 'the same thing over and over again' – like a photo album – and providing 'views of one object seen from different angles' (CV 7/9).[191] The preface to the *Investigations* uses much the same wording: 'The same or almost the same points were always being approached afresh from different directions, and new sketches made.'

Each attempt by later Wittgenstein to create a book for his philosopher reader included an attempt at offering a perspicuous representation of the multifarious depth grammar of language, and thus to offer the reader a way to see the multiple and complex connections within language (§122). The goal may have remained largely the same, but the model for each such perspicuous representation changed. The different manifestations of Wittgenstein's book project hence show different conceptions of how perspicuous representation is

---

[189] Pichler 2018. [190] Schopenhauer 1873: Vorrede. [191] See also Anscombe 1969: 376.

to be practised. Is it the author Wittgenstein or rather the reader who is to 'find and invent the intermediate links' (§122), and thus also to fill in the gaps from one case to the other? In a *Bemerkungen only* variant of the book, the reader is left entirely to their own devices for finding and seeing the connections. In the *Brown Book* variant, on the other hand, Wittgenstein tries to do most of the work *for* the reader. The reader doesn't need to walk by themselves in uncharted terrain; Wittgenstein guides them through the map and tries to illuminate *for* the reader the dark spots of the map bit by bit and fill in all the gaps. Moreover, the *Brown Book* and the *Betrachtung* each have a specific beginning on which they depend. But already in the *Yellow Book* Wittgenstein rightly stated with reference to Schopenhauer: philosophy is 'an organism', and it should 'not matter where I begin' (YB §1; DPS 104).[192] Spengler's organic development from birth to death is consequently transformed into an organic structure that has no stages or levels, and no birth and no end.

With the *Investigations* album, then, the reader is encouraged to walk by themselves, with the precipitate from Wittgenstein's own earlier philosophical walks as their guide. Here the reader does not receive a book with aphorisms or also just *Bemerkungen,* nor a book which followed or imposed a strict and overly systematising order. In the *Tractatus* Wittgenstein had sought to offer a summary of it through the cardinal propositions, but the *Investigations* no longer aims to offer a summary. Instead, the *Investigations* gives the reader examples of doing philosophy from which they could proceed to develop their own ways of clarifying concepts and problems – as well as clarifying their philosophical self. In 1949, Wittgenstein said to Drury: 'Every sentence in the *Tractatus* should be seen as the heading of a chapter, needing further exposition. My present style is quite different; I am trying to avoid that error' (MDC 159). In the *Investigations* the reader is to produce the apt perspicuous representations on their own during the journey. This chimes in with Wittgenstein saying in the preface: 'I should not like my writing to spare other people the trouble of thinking.' It also echoes his earlier saying from 1931 that he is to be only a 'mirror' for his reader (CV 18/25). Eventually, according to Cavell, the reader's following will require 'a willingness to recognize in oneself the moments of strangeness, sickness, disappointment, self-destructiveness, perversity, suffocation, torment, lostness that are articulated in the language of the *Investigations*' – but also 'to recognize in its philosophizing that its pleasures ... will lie in the specific forms and moments of self-recovery it proposes ...'.[193] Perspicuous representation thus becomes, as much as a project of discovering the grammar of 'the primitive fact of ordinary language', an

---

[192] See also Venturinha 2013: 7 and Savickey 2017: 24.   [193] Cavell 2004: 27.

existential project of finding clarity about one's own philosophical self.[194] Wittgenstein's book needed a form that fully lent itself to this deeply Socratic purpose.[195]

The *Investigations*' album format was already strongly announced in November 1930. The book that presents the reader a 'mirror' of their own philosophical character, aspirations and deeds is a better book than one which doesn't. In doing so, it permits the reader to enter at any point, and each reader to enter in a way such that their specific hic et nunc perspectives are acknowledged. The *Brown Book* did not live up to this expectation. In fact, it largely spared the reader the trouble of finding their ways through grammar. Instead, there the reader could follow the path Wittgenstein had drawn up for them on the map. But with such an arrangement, the reader acquired much less of a competence of walking in uncharted terrain than was needed. Without that competence, they might easily get lost when coming from a different direction or starting at a different point (cf. §203). With the *Investigations*, Wittgenstein wants his readers to confront these features already when reading his book. From his own activity of clarification, he knows that a philosophical problem cannot necessarily be attacked straight on. His train of thought involved many repetitive movements, and while it created a lot of motion, it proceeded only little by little (Ms-110,82; 1931). Usually, he also had to sneak around the problem before he could get close to it (Ms-118,77r-77v; 1937). He seeks to give his readers this same kind of experience in the *Investigations*.

3.6 Poetry versus Drivel

Wittgenstein thinks that philosophy, be it in the activity of original philosophical clarification or in the effort of creating the book apt for the reader, is ultimately to bring in forms and tools that are at home in poetry. It is only poetry which can offer, in perfectionist form, the *full* palette of literary means and methods that philosophy is to make use of for moving one's thoughts: comparison, analogy, simile, picture, metaphor, story, thought experiment, narrative fiction, dialogue, irony, prosody, to mention only a few. If formal argument had been *all* that there is to philosophy, then the *Investigations* would not require either the specific album form or more generally the use of poetry. But for Wittgenstein, formal argument is only *one* of the many different tools to be put to work in philosophy. Therefore, he opposes Carnap, who wants to ban the poetic from philosophy.[196]

---

[194] Cavell 2004: 29.
[195] See also Wallgren 2006: ch. 7; Sunday Grève 2015 and Savickey 2017: 135–6.
[196] Carnap 1961: xix (1967: xvi-xvii).

For Wittgenstein, the combination of philosophy and poetry does not involve any opposition to philosophical argument, and the attention to style in philosophy does not involve any opposition to clarity. Indeed, the opposite is the case: argument and clarity depend on style, and Wittgenstein's stylistic aspirations are therefore at the same time philosophical aspirations.[197] However, combining philosophy and poetry does not imply that *all* means and forces mobilised in literature would also be conducive to philosophy. The maxim *No drivel!* is still valid. It applies to poetry in philosophy, as also to poetry *itself*. There is no straight road that leads from being poetic to engaging in idle talk and drivel. Kraus would think that poetry is the place where no words are wasted. This is what permitted Wittgenstein to say about the *Tractatus*: 'The work is strictly philosophical and, at the same time, literary, but there is no babbling in it.'[198] And what permitted the later Wittgenstein to state that the language-game is the ideal end point for cutting out philosophical excess and ornament, for 'the essence of the language-game is a practical method (a way of acting) – not speculation, not chatter' (CE 421). In fact, the maxim *No drivel!* applies for Wittgenstein to *any* writing, including writing of personal notes (see MT 105: 'don't blather!'). No one understood Wittgenstein better on this point than Engelmann. Still, Wittgenstein thought that even Engelmann, with his dramatic ode 'Orpheus', fell victim to drivel (Ms-111,196–200; 1931).

Wittgenstein's linking of philosophy to poetry could then well have been informed by Kraus' view that it is only in imaginative poetry ('Dichtung') that language is put to work properly and in a perfectly clean and clear manner:[199] philosophy requires as much care as goes into writing a poem (cf. CV 24/28). Poetry is for Kraus the *opposite* of drivel and careless language. This reflects the view that philosophy for Wittgenstein was as much an ethical as a logical or grammatical undertaking. He wants the philosopher to achieve *justice* ('Gerechtigkeit') to the facts, and thus brings into play moral qualities. This ties in with Weininger's thoughts about logic and ethics ultimately being one and the same.[200] Kraus and Weininger may have inspired Wittgenstein to continuously remind himself that a mistake in language may not only be the *manifestation* of an ethical failure, but may also amount to an ethical failure itself.[201] One point of the *Investigations'* critique of Augustine's account of language is precisely about faulty ethics rather than faulty cognition; the ethical fault in question is the attitude of neglect towards all language that is not names and naming. This does not exclude the possibility that the neglect may itself again be rooted in a grammatical misunderstanding of the functioning of names.

---

[197] Cf. Glock (forthcoming).
[198] To von Ficker, around 7.10.1919 (CLF 94; see also CLF 95).   [199] Savickey 2017: 42–3.
[200] Weininger 1904: 200.   [201] Kraus 1910.

Engelmann stresses the moral importance which Kraus attributes to the use of the comma (CPE 127). Again, there seem to be few other philosophers who subject their punctuation and style to critical scrutiny more than Wittgenstein. Loos too makes the connection between style and ethics, and his opposition to unnecessary ornament in craftsmanship is mirrored in Wittgenstein's careful editing of his texts. If Wittgenstein had to decide between alternative phrasings, he would usually choose the less ornamental one.[202] Many have attested that Wittgenstein's search for asceticism in philosophy was matched by a search for the same in Wittgenstein the man: 'He spoke with great simplicity and compelling earnestness, in faultless English, conveying an instantaneous impression of intellectual integrity and moral force.'[203] Loos wants craft to produce ornamentless, but functional objects; this demands skill rather than art and the artistic.[204] Wittgenstein's idea that philosophy 'is reduced to a matter of skill' (LC 5:2) fits in here perfectly.

Kraus might well have exerted an important influence on another level too. If Frege was the one from whom Wittgenstein adapted the ideal of gapless sequence, Kraus might in contrast have inspired and encouraged Wittgenstein to make the leap to the album which permits gaps. Kraus' magnum opus *The Last Days of Mankind*[205] presents a collage of loosely connected scenes and fragments with quotations. Moreover, in contrast to a piece with a strong presence of authorial voice, it lets the protagonists speak for themselves, thereby permitting the author to take a step back and 'only describe' (§124). Kraus' opus simply puts things on stage, indeed puts a polyphonic scenery on stage. At the same time, no one could say that Kraus didn't get his message across, bringing to the fore the deep deficiencies and immoralities of his protagonists or their contexts.

3.7 Belief in the Poetic Genius

Wittgenstein's remark about the link between philosophy and poetry must also be traced back to Frege, Spengler and Ernst. Wittgenstein says in the summer of 1929 that his way of doing philosophy essentially consists in a transition from asking about truth to asking about sense (Ms-105,46). This correlates with a distinction Frege makes between science ('Wissenschaft') and poetry ('Dichtung').[206] Wittgenstein himself opposes the two in RPP II §92 (originating from December 1947). Science seeks to establish truth, ideally by way of logical inferences and proofs; poetry seeks to establish sense, often by

---

[202] See Somavilla 2015: 130 and Pichler 2020: 115.   [203] Leach 2020: 218.
[204] See also Long 2020 ('strategy of sorting') and Westergaard 1995 (on Loos' *Raumplanung*).
[205] Kraus 1922.   [206] Frege 1918: 63 (1997: 330); see Gabriel 2018 and Bengtsson 2018.

proceeding along analogies, metaphors and similes. Most significantly, elucidations are for Frege part of poetry rather than an expression of science. Wittgenstein's remark about the link between philosophy and poetry can thus be read as: if philosophy is to choose between science and poetry, it is to go with poetry. This is supported by Spengler, for whom culture, history and philosophy are to be handled 'poetically' rather than 'causally', or in the way subjects of science are handled.[207] But poetry, Spengler thinks, has disappeared from this age of civilisation, and the literary giants of his times try 'to shape tragedy *causally* ... they do not sing [*dichten*]'.[208] This may shed light on Wittgenstein's thought that his attitude ('Stellung'; CV 24/28) to philosophy as poetry 'must reveal how far my thinking belongs to the present, the future, or the past' (CV 24/28). To the extent it succeeds in being poetry following Spengler's stipulation, Wittgenstein's philosophy belongs to the past and will still be *culture*. But Wittgenstein following Spengler in distinguishing between 'culture' and 'civilization'[209] thinks he 'cannot quite do what he would like to be able to do' (CV 24/28), and therefore his philosophy may after all bear more the mark of the present than of the past, and thus be *civilisation*. What it is that he feels he 'cannot quite do' may well have to do with falling short of the ideal that Ernst puts up for poetry ('Dichtungen'): 'we should feel them, take them in and let them work in us'.[210] Already in the *Tractatus* preface Wittgenstein said that one of the two values of the book consisted in the fact 'that in it thoughts are expressed, and this value will be the greater the better the thoughts are expressed. ... Here I am conscious that I have fallen far short of the possible' (Ramsey-Ogden translation). From this perspective, Wittgenstein's philosophy can be seen to live in the tension between art and skill. This becomes even clearer when we look at Schopenhauer who, like Weininger, affiliated philosophy with genius rather than with talent.

For Schopenhauer, philosophy both starts from and appeals to intuition ('Anschauung'). Schopenhauer says further that strong intuition, thinking in pictures and imagination ('Phantasie') are what characterise the *genius*. As such, philosophy belongs together with poetry ('Poesie') rather than with abstract thinking.[211] If philosophy's perspicuous representation is about finding or inventing intermediate links so that the understanding can come about 'which consists in "seeing connections"' (§122), then it is phantasy, storytelling and poetry at its best that are needed for not only inventing the missing links but also weaving the elements together in such a way that the connections can be easily

---

[207] Spengler 1920: 139: ' ... über Geschichte soll man *dichten*' (1927: 96; my italics).
[208] Spengler 1927: 156 (1920: 213).
[209] See for example CV 6–8/8–10; see also von Wright 1982: 201–16. [210] Ernst 1910: 271.
[211] Schopenhauer 1873: vol. II, ch. 31.

seen. But perspicuous representation can become more than just a method applied for addressing specific philosophical problems; as it grows into an attitude and way of looking at the world such that one tries to see and find the connections everywhere and continuously, it amounts to a *Weltanschauung* (§122). Ernst demonstrated masterfully in his *Nachwort*, contrasting the act of copying nature ('Naturnachahmung') with poetic creativity, how through finding and inventing connecting links between the motives and stories of fairy tales not only these but also our own feelings and conceptual schemes can be connected. One example is his discussion of Aeschylus' *Oresteia*.[212] Indeed, there Ernst showed 'a complicated network of similarities overlapping and criss-crossing: similarities in the large and in the small' (§66). It is in this context that Ernst used the term 'Sprachlogik': it is the logic of the past which often is no longer understood, but which we should try to connect with through the invention of intermediate links.[213] Naturally, this can result in *misunderstanding* (Ms-110,184; 20.6.1931).

In contrast to the poetic genius shown by Ernst stands one who is merely gifted. The gifted one is endowed with *talent* that is confined to making use of discursive rational thinking, theoretical concepts and learned skill.[214] Wittgenstein concedes that he is only a 'second-rate poet', and thinks that it might therefore be better if he quit trying to create poetry ('Dichten', Ms-117,193; 1940). He is 'someone who cannot quite do what he would like to be able to do' (CV 24/28). He considers himself to have mainly talent only, although possibly with some 'flashes of genius' (CV 65/75). Manifestations of flashes of genius might have been to him literary images, and such 'gestures as these: "What is your aim in philosophy?" "To show the fly the way out of the fly-bottle" (§309); "Why can't my right hand give my left hand money?" (§268); "We have got on to slippery ice where there is no friction and so in a certain sense the conditions are ideal but also, just because of that, we are unable to walk" (§107)'.[215] Each of these are ways of convincing that do their work 'without the means or intermediary methods of grammatical investigations' and discursive procedure only.[216] He thought that many admired figures had talent only, although possibly with some 'flashes of genius', for example 'Freud, Spengler, Kraus, Einstein' (CV -/53) and Mendelssohn (CV 38–9/43–4).[217] It needs, according to Weininger, a person with genius to do philosophy properly, and it is only the philosopher and the artist, not the scientist or the skilled

---

[212] See Ernst 1910: 290, 292, 295.
[213] Ernst 1910: 308: 'indem eine spätere Zeit die Sprachlogik der Vergangenheit nicht mehr verstand und durch Erfindungen deutete'.
[214] Schopenhauer 1873: vol. II, ch. 31.   [215] Cavell 2004: 24.   [216] Cavell 2004: 24.
[217] See also CV 18–19/16, 47–50/53–57, 53/61, 67/76–77 and 75–76/86.

scholar, who deserve to be called a genius.[218] Wittgenstein himself states that the work of philosophical clarification requires *courage*; 'without this it becomes a mere clever game' (CV 19/16). We need to see this together with his conviction that it is the *genius* that is characterised by courage (CV 18–9/16, 35/40, 36/42 *et passim*).

Thus, while Wittgenstein *does* conceive of himself as an artist and a poet, he regards himself as a 'a second-rate artist'[219] and a 'second-rate poet' only, and as a writer with talent only. As such he finds himself ultimately forced to write and form philosophy in the hard way, using cleverness and skill: labouring; searching for words; struggling for the right phrasing; polishing and polishing; working hard on getting right the concepts, arguments, similes, thought experiments and so on; selecting, arranging and re-arranging; continuously editing and re-editing – 'a mode of writing that depended on constant revision'.[220] In contrast, the 'great' genius (CV -/53), the genius giant, with whom Wittgenstein constantly and with despair compares himself, can create the right expression out of 'poetic mood' (CV 65–6/75), poetic immediacy, and 'express himself perfectly' (CV 71/81). The genius is *original*, whereas the one with mere talent lives by learning from and *imitating* the original (MT 131). Even Wittgenstein's use of the expression 'precipitate' in the preface to the *Investigations* connects with Schopenhauer. Schopenhauer writes that mastery 'in poetry [*Dichtung*] as in chemistry, enables us always to obtain the precise precipitate [*Niederschlag*] we intended'.[221] One task pertaining to the composition of the *Investigations* consisted in rightly *forming* the precipitate from philosophising. This act, in order to be successful, must be an act of poetry proper. Only if it becomes an act of poetry can it create the optimal setting for the philosophical precipitate to settle in and take the shape conducive to the reader.

Plato, Nietzsche and Schopenhauer might have been representatives of philosophers of the past for Wittgenstein; Russell, Moore and Carnap were representatives of the present. According to Carnap, the future of philosophy belonged to philosophy *without* poetry. Furthermore, Carnap had explicitly associated the attitude ('Haltung') of the philosopher of the past with the attitude of the poet ('Dichter').[222] Spengler held that Western culture had come to its final stage, namely: *civilisation*. In the 'preface' remarks from November 1930 Wittgenstein voiced his feeling of distance from the spirit of Western civilisation. This spirit was, he thought, the spirit of *progress* which found expression in 'the industry, architecture, music, of present day' as well as in 'fascism & socialism' (CV 6/8). It also found expression in a philosophy

---

[218] Weininger 1904: 219.   [219] Anscombe 1969: 373, 375.   [220] Perloff 2004: 41.
[221] Schopenhauer 1873 (1969): vol. I, book 3, §5.   [222] Carnap 1961: xix (1967: xvi).

which makes linear progress its principle. Wittgenstein contrasts such philosophy with the spirit of his own work: 'One movement orders one thought to the others in a series, the other keeps aiming at the same place. One movement constructs & takes (in hand) one stone after another, the other keeps reaching for the same one' (CV 7/10). These phrasings again allude to Carnap who states in his preface: 'Thus stone will be carefully added to stone and a safe building will be erected' (xvii). Carnap's preface to *Logischer Aufbau der Welt* encapsulated for Wittgenstein the spirit of progress in civilisation. Where Carnap wanted linearity and series, Wittgenstein eventually insisted on adhering to the criss-cross album. Even the motto of the *Investigations* makes the spirit of linear progress in philosophy an object of criticism. Already in September 1930 Wittgenstein had, in critical opposition to the first issue of the journal *Erkenntnis*, cautioned Schlick with the line from Nestroy.[223] Therefore, Wittgenstein may have thought that a philosophy *without* poetry is philosophy in the age of civilisation, but also felt that *his* vision of philosophy adhered to the past age of *culture*. That he 'cannot quite do what he would like to be able to do' (CV 24/28) will then also have to do with the fact that he no longer lives in an age of culture.

With regard to Nietzsche, Wittgenstein discovered in April 1938 (Ms-120,145r) that there was a twofold connection between his philosophy and Nietzsche's. First, like Nietzsche, he doesn't want to teach a more correct thinking in old parameters, but different and new ways of thinking and proceeding ('Gedankenbewegung'). These new ways are of such a scope that only the Nietzschean phrase 'transvaluation of values' ('Umwertung von Werten') captures the dimension of the change. Second, he finds himself intimately connected to Nietzsche through his thought that the philosopher needs to be a poet. Wittgenstein showed great respect for the philosophical potential of poets and remarked: 'People nowadays think, scientists are there to instruct them, poets, musicians etc. to entertain them. *That the latter have something to teach them*; that never occurs to them' (CV 36/42). Of Busch he said: 'He has the real philosophical urge' (ICE: To Rhees 22.1.1950; see, for example, Busch's *Eduards Traum*).[224]

The philosophical transvaluation that Wittgenstein implied requires a transformation in the person. Such a change in the reader could be brought about in two ways. The first way is described in Wittgenstein's Cambridge lecture of 13 October 1930, where he says that philosophy is now reduced to a matter of skill and that the way to acquire the skill required for philosophy is *discussion* (LC 5:2). This path calls for long exercise which, if successful, yields

---

[223] To Schlick 18.9.1930 (Iven 2015: 119–20); see also von Wright 1993: 209 and Nyíri 1976.
[224] See Rothhaupt 2009; McGuinness 2010; Biesenbach 2014; Janik 2018 and Somavilla 2020.

skill and mastery of craftsmanship.[225] We can associate this route with Loos. The second path is not artifice, but it is art. More precisely, it is the art of the genius working through poetry. We can associate this route with Schopenhauer, Weininger and Spengler, who all held that philosophy needs the great poet, rather than a person with only skill and talent. For Wittgenstein the second way seemed still possible, and possibly also necessary. When discussing how philosophy should be done, he vacillated between the two ways. When embarking on the first path, the Wittgenstein reader can rely on learning from the countless minute philosophical discussions they encounter in Wittgenstein's *Nachlass*. There they find Wittgenstein's own philosophical reactions, often already in poetic form. With regard to the second, Wittgenstein wished to offer the reader also a philosophical book out of the precipitate from these reactions, in poetic composition. With it, he hoped, the reader could be changed by, as Schopenhauer put it, poetic elevation ('Erhebung').[226] Ultimately, Wittgenstein hoped to help make the philosophical reader as also himself 'see the world aright' again. The most powerful means to make us, even his modern readers, 'look at the whole business in a different way' (WCL 168) is often the poetic picture, as Wittgenstein realised through his own clarifications.

It can be a confession that powerfully marks the beginning of the change in the person. Wittgenstein writes in the preface to his *Investigations* that they 'could be seen in the right light only by contrast with and against the background of my old way of thinking'. He then begins the book with a quote from Augustine's *Confessions* and goes on to lay out and deal with the philosophical sins of the *Tractatus*. However, this Element has tried to show that the *Investigations* is, with its album and criss-cross rather than linear and gapless sequence form, to be seen in contrast not only to the *Tractatus* but also the *Brown Book*. The contrasts between the three are strongly visible in, and connected with, the different styles and forms each of the three works took. In each of the three, style, method and content make up a specific unit which represents Wittgenstein's philosophy at the time. To achieve in both style and content, the perfect book and not only 'a good book' (Preface), Wittgenstein thought he would have needed much more than talent, indeed he would need poetic genius. A third meaning of the statement about the link between philosophy and poetry is hence that, according to Wittgenstein, philosophy proper can, and therefore also should, really only be done by the poetic genius. But this requires adherence to (an age of) *culture*; without culture, any philosophical author will have to *struggle* like he did, and fall terribly short of the task.

---

[225] Rhees to von Wright 22.1.1976: 'lange Übung'; cited after Erbacher 2019: 131.

[226] Schopenhauer 1873: vol. I, §§37–41 *et passim*; vol. II, ch. 37.

Wittgenstein felt that his philosophy lived in the tension between civilisation and skill on the one hand, and culture and art on the other. At the same time, he wondered whether his 'cultural ideal' was not 'from the time of Schumann', but actually 'a new one' (CV 2/4). At least he could hope that 'one day a culture will arise out of this civilization' (CV 64/73).

References

Wittgenstein Primary Sources Cited by Abbreviation

BBB (1969) *Preliminary Studies for the 'Philosophical Investigations'*. Generally known as The *Blue* and *Brown Books*. Rush Rhees (ed.), Oxford: Blackwell

BNE (2015) *Wittgenstein Source Bergen Nachlass Edition*. Wittgenstein Archives at the University of Bergen under the direction of Alois Pichler (ed.). In *Wittgenstein Source* (2009), curated by Alois Pichler (2009) and Joseph Wang-Kathrein (2020) (wittgensteinsource.org). Bergen: Wittgenstein Archives at the University of Bergen

BT (2005) *The Big Typescript: TS 213*. C. Grant Luckhardt, M. A. E. Aue (eds., trans.). Oxford: Blackwell

CCO (1973) *Letters to C. K. Ogden with Comments on the English Translation of the Tractatus Logico-Philosophicus*. G. H. von Wright (ed.). Oxford: Basil Blackwell

CE (1976) Ursache und Wirkung: Intuitives Erfassen/Cause and Effect: Intuitive Awareness. In J. C. Klagge, A. Nordmann (eds.), *Ludwig Wittgenstein: Philosophical Occasions 1912–1951*. Indianapolis: Hackett, 370–426

CLF (1996) Letters to Ludwig von Ficker. A. Janik (ed.), B. Gillette (trans.). In C. G. Luckhardt (ed.), *Wittgenstein: Sources and Perspectives*. Bristol: Thoemmes Press, 82–98.

CPE (1967) Engelmann, P.: Briefe von Wittgenstein/Letters from Wittgenstein. In B. F. McGuinness (ed.), L. Furtmüller (trans.), *Letters from Ludwig Wittgenstein: With a Memoir*. Oxford: Blackwell, 2–59

CV (1980) *Vermischte Bemerkungen: Eine Auswahl aus dem Nachlaß/ Culture and Value: A Selection from the Posthumous Remains*. G. H. von Wright in collaboration with H. Nyman (eds.), Peter Winch (trans.). Oxford: Blackwell

CV (1998) *Vermischte Bemerkungen: Eine Auswahl aus dem Nachlaß/Culture and Value: A Selection from the Posthumous Remains*. G. H. von Wright in cooperation with H. Nyman, revised by A. Pichler (eds.), Peter Winch (trans.). Oxford: Blackwell

DPS (2020) *Ludwig Wittgenstein: Dictating Philosophy to Francis Skinner – The Wittgenstein-Skinner Manuscripts*. A. Gibson, N. O'Mahony (eds.), Cham: Springer

EPB (1984) *Eine Philosophische Betrachtung.* R. Rhees (ed.). In Suhrkamp-Werkausgabe Vol. 5. Frankfurt a. M.: Suhrkamp, 117–282

ICE (2013) *Gesamtbriefwechsel: Innsbrucker elektronische Ausgabe.* B. McGuinness, J. Wang (eds.), Im Auftrag des Forschungsinstituts Brenner-Archiv. Charlottesville (Virginia): InteLex

LA (1966) *Lectures and Conversations.* C. Barrett (ed.), Oxford: Basil Blackwell

LC (2016) *Wittgenstein: Lectures, Cambridge 1930–1933: From the Notes of G. E. Moore.* D. Stern, B. Rogers, G. Citron (eds.), Cambridge: Cambridge University Press

LFM (1976) *Wittgenstein's Lectures on the Foundations of Mathematics: Cambridge, 1939.* C. Diamond (ed.), Chicago: The University of Chicago Press

LPA (2016) *Wittgenstein Source Facsimile Edition of Tractatus Publication Materials.* Alfred Schmidt (ed.), In Wittgenstein Source (2009), curated by Alois Pichler (2009) and Joseph Wang-Kathrein (2020) [wittgensteinsource.org]. Bergen: Wittgenstein Archives at the University of Bergen

LPE (1993) Notes for Lectures on 'Private Experience' and 'Sense Data'. D. G. Stern (ed.). In J. C. Klagge, A. Nordmann (eds.), *Ludwig Wittgenstein: Philosophical Occasions 1912–1951.* Indianapolis: Hackett, 200–88

MDC (1984) Drury, M. O'C.: Conversations with Wittgenstein. In R. Rhees (ed.), *Recollections of Wittgenstein.* Oxford: Oxford University Press, 97–171

MDN (1984) Drury, M. O'C.: Some Notes on Conversations with Wittgenstein. In R. Rhees (ed.), *Recollections of Wittgenstein.* Oxford: Oxford University Press, 76–96

MT (2003) Movements of Thought: Diaries, 1930–1932, 1936–1937. I. Somavilla (ed.). In J. C. Klagge, A. Nordmann (eds.), A. Nordmann (trans.), *Ludwig Wittgenstein: Public and Private Occasions.* Lanham: Rowman and Littlefield, 3–255

OC (1969) *Über Gewißheit/On Certainty.* G. E. M. Anscombe, G. H. von Wright (eds.), D. Paul, G. E. M. Anscombe (trans.). Oxford: Blackwell

PG (1974) *Philosophical Grammar.* R. Rhees (ed.), A. Kenny (trans.). Oxford: Blackwell

PR (1975) *Philosophical Remarks.* R. Rhees (ed.), R. Hargreaves, R. White (trans.). Oxford: Blackwell

PI (1953) *Philosophische Untersuchungen/Philosophical Investigations.* G. E. M. Anscombe, R. Rhees (eds.), G. E. M. Anscombe (trans.). Oxford: Blackwell

PI (2009) *Philosophische Untersuchungen/Philosophical Investigations*. P. M. S. Hacker, J. Schulte (eds.), G. E. M. Anscombe, P. M. S. Hacker, J. Schulte (trans.). New York: Wiley

RFM (1978) *Remarks on the Foundations of Mathematics*. G. H. von Wright, R. Rhees, G. E. M. Anscombe (eds.), G. E. M. Anscombe (trans.). Oxford: Blackwell

TLP (1961) *Tractatus Logico-Philosophicus*. D. F. Pears, B. F. McGuinness (trans.). London: Routledge and Kegan Paul

WC (2008) *Wittgenstein in Cambridge: Letters and Documents 1911–1951*. B. McGuinness (ed.). Oxford: Blackwell

WCL (2017) *Wittgenstein's Whewell's Court Lectures Cambridge 1938–1941: From the Notes by Yorick Smythies*. Volker A. Munz, B. Ritter (eds.). Oxford: Wiley

WWK (1979) *Ludwig Wittgenstein and the Vienna Circle: Conversations recorded by F. Waismann*. B. F. McGuinness (ed.), J. Schulte, B. F. McGuinness (trans.). Oxford: Blackwell

YB (1979) The Yellow Book (Selected Parts). In A. Ambrose (ed.), *Wittgenstein's Lectures: Cambridge, 1932–1935*. Oxford: Blackwell, 41–73

Z (1981) *Zettel*. G. E. M. Anscombe, G. H. von Wright (eds.), G. E. M. Anscombe (trans.). Oxford: Blackwell

Primary Sources

Bakhtin, M. (1984) *Problems of Dostoevsky's Poetics*. C. Emerson (ed., trans.). London: University of Minnesota Press

Boltzmann, L. (1979) *Populäre Schriften*. E. Broda (ed.). Braunschweig: Friedr. Vieweg und Sohn

Busch, W. (1891) *Eduards Traum*. München: Bassermann

Carnap, R. (1961) *Der Logische Aufbau der Welt*. Leipzig: Felix Meiner

Carnap, R. (1967) *The Logical Structure of the World*. R. A. George (trans.). London: Routledge

Carroll, L. (1865) *Alice's Adventures in Wonderland*. London: Macmillan

Ernst, P. (1910) Nachwort zu Kinder- und Hausmärchen. Gesammelt durch die Brüder Grimm. In: *Kinder- und Hausmärchen; Gesammelt durch die Brüder Grimm*. München: Georg Müller. Vol. 3, 271–314

Frege, G. (1884) *Die Grundlagen der Arithmetik: Eine logisch-mathematische Untersuchung über den Begriff der Zahl*. Breslau: W. Koebner

Frege, G. (1893) *Grundgesetze der Arithmetik: Begriffsschriftlich abgeleitet* (vol. 1, 1903 vol. 2). Jena: Hermann Pohle

Frege, G. (1906) Über die Grundlagen der Geometrie [2nd series]. *Jahresbericht der Deutschen Mathematiker-Vereinigung* 15, 293–309, 377–403, 423–30

Frege, G. (1918) Der Gedanke: Eine logische Untersuchung. *Beiträge zur Philosophie des deutschen Idealismus* I(2), 58–77

Frege, G. (1960) *Translations from the Philosophical Writings of Gottlob Frege.* P. T. Geach (trans.). Oxford: Basil Blackwell

Frege, G. (1974) *The Foundations of Arithmetic: A Logico-Mathematical Enquiry into the Concept of Number.* J. L. Austin (trans.). Oxford: Blackwell

Frege, G. (1984) *Collected Papers on Mathematics, Logic, and Philosophy.* B. McGuinness (ed.), M. Black, V. H. Dudman, P. Geach et al. (trans.). Oxford: Blackwell, 293–340

Frege, G. (1997) *The Frege Reader.* M. Beaney (ed.). Oxford: Blackwell.

Hertz, H. (1894) *Die Prinzipien der Mechanik in neuem Zusammenhange dargestellt.* Leipzig: Johann Ambrosius Barth

Kierkegaard, S. (1941) *Concluding Unscientific Postscript.* D. F. Swenson, W. Lowrie (trans.). Princeton: Princeton University Press

Kraus, K. (1910) *Heine und die Folgen.* München: Albert Langen

Kraus, K. (1922) *Die letzten Tage der Menschheit.* Wien: Die Fackel

Loos, A. (1929) Ornament und Verbrechen. *Frankfurter Zeitung* 24 October. https://de.wikisource.org/wiki/Ornament_und_Verbrechen

Malinowski, B. (1923) The Problem of Meaning in Primitive Languages. In C. K. Ogden, I. A. Richards (eds.), *The Meaning of Meaning.* London: Kegan Paul, Trench, Trübner, 296–336

Ramsey, F. P. (1990) *Philosophical Papers.* D. H. Mellor (ed.). Cambridge: Cambridge University Press

Russell, B. (1914) *Our Knowledge of the External World as a Field for Scientific Method in Philosophy.* Chicago: Open Court

Schopenhauer, A. (1873) *Die Welt als Wille und Vorstellung* (vol. 1 and 2). Leipzig: Brockhaus

Schopenhauer, A. (1969) *The World as Will and Representation* (vol. 1 and 2). E. F. J. Payne (trans.). New York: Dover

Spengler, O. (1920) *Der Untergang des Abendlandes: Umrisse einer Morphologie der Weltgeschichte. Erster Band: Gestalt und Wirklichkeit* (vol. 1). München: C. H. Beck

Spengler, O. (1927) *The Decline of the West* (vol. 1 and 2). Ch. F. Atkinson (trans.). New York: Alfred A. Knopf

Sraffa, P. (1960) *The Production of Commodities by Means of Commodities.* Cambridge: Cambridge University Press

Waismann, F. (1976) *Logik, Sprache, Philosophie*. G. P. Baker, B. McGuinness (eds.). Stuttgart: Philipp Reclam jun.

Weininger, O. (1904) G*eschlecht und Charakter: Eine prinzipielle Untersuchung*. Wien: W. Braumüller

Secondary Sources

Andrews, D. R. (1996) Nothing is Hidden: A Wittgensteinian Interpretation of Sraffa. *Cambridge Journal of Economics* 20:6, 763–77

Anscombe, G. E. M. (1969) On the Form of Wittgenstein's Writing. In R. Klibansky (ed.), *Contemporary Philosophy/La Philosophie Contemporaine*, III. Firenze: La Nuova Italia, 373–8

Appelqvist, H. (2018) Wittgenstein on Aesthetic Normativity and Grammar. In D. Stern (ed.), *Wittgenstein in the 1930s: Between the Tractatus and the Investigations*. Cambridge: Cambridge University Press, 209–23

Baker, G. P., Hacker, P. M. S. (2005a) *Wittgenstein: Understanding and Meaning. Part I: Essays*, 2nd ed., Oxford: Blackwell

Baker, G. P., Hacker, P. M. S. (2005b) *Wittgenstein: Understanding and Meaning. Part II: Exegesis §§1–184*, 2nd ed., Oxford: Blackwell

Bazzocchi, L. (ed.) (2014) *The Tractatus According to Its Own Form*. Raleigh: Lulu

Bengtsson, G. (2018) Frege on Dichtung and Elucidation. In G. Bengtsson, S. Säätelä and A. Pichler (eds.), *New Essays on Frege: Between Science and Literature*. Cham: Springer, 101–17

Biesenbach, H. (2014) *Anspielungen und Zitate im Werk Ludwig Wittgensteins*. Sofia: Sofia University Press

Biggs, M. A. R. (1998) Wittgenstein: Graphics, Normativity and Paradigms. In H. W. Krüger, A. Pichler (eds.), *Arbeiten zu Wittgenstein*. Bergen: Wittgenstein Archives at the University of Bergen, 8–22

Brusotti, M. (2016) Ethnologische Betrachtungsweisen: Wittgenstein, Frazer, Sraffa. *Wittgenstein-Studien* 7:1, 39–63

Brusotti, M. (2018) What Belongs to a Language Game is a Whole Culture: On Two Related Concepts in Wittgenstein's Philosophy. *Wittgenstein-Studien* 9:1, 51–73

Cavell, St. (1966) The Availability of Wittgenstein's Later Philosophy. In G. Pitcher (ed.), *Wittgenstein: The Philosophical Investigations*. New York: Doubleday, 151–85

Cavell, St. (2004) The Investigations' Everyday Aesthetics of Itself. In J. Gibson, W. Huemer (eds.), *The Literary Wittgenstein*. London: Routledge, 21–33

Cerný, L. (1972) Essay. In J. Ritter (ed.), *Historisches Wörterbuch der Philosophie*, Vol. 2. Basel: Schwabe, 746–9

Conant, J. (1997) Kierkegaard's Postscript and Wittgenstein's Tractatus: Teaching How to Pass from Disguised to Patent Nonsense. *Wittgenstein-Studien* 2, 11–2–97.TXT

Conant, J. (2011) Wittgenstein's Methods. In O. Kuusela, M. McGinn (eds.) *The Oxford Handbook of Wittgenstein*. Oxford: Oxford University Press, 620–45

De Iaco, M. (2018) A List of Meetings between Wittgenstein and Sraffa. *Nordic Wittgenstein Review* 7:1, 83–99

De Iaco, M. (2019) Wittgenstein to Sraffa: Two Newly-Discovered Letters from February and March 1934. *Nordic Wittgenstein Review* 8:1–2, 209–23

Décultot, E. (2014). Dichtung. In B. Cassin (ed.), *A Dictionary of Untranslatables: A Philosophical Lexicon*. Princeton: Princeton University Press

Diamond, C. (1991) *The Realistic Spirit*. Cambridge: MIT Press

Engelmann, M. L. (2013) *Wittgenstein's Philosophical Development: Phenomenology, Grammar, Method, and the Anthropological View*. Basingstoke: Palgrave Macmillan

Engelmann, M. L. (2016) The Faces of 'Necessity', Perspicuous Representation, and the Irreligious 'Cult of the Useful'. In L. Albinus, J. G. F. Rothhaupt, A. Seery (eds.), *Wittgenstein's Remarks on Frazer: The Text and the Matter*. Berlin: De Gruyter, 129–74

Erbacher, Chr. (2015) *Formen des Klärens: Literarisch-philosophische. Darstellungsmittel in Wittgensteins Schriften*. Münster: Mentis

Erbacher, Chr. (2019) 'Good' Philosophical Reasons for 'Bad' Editorial Philology? On Rhees and Wittgenstein's *Philosophical Grammar*. *Philosophical Investigations* 42:2, 111–45

Erbacher, Chr. , dos Santos Reis, A., Jung, J. (2019) 'Ludwig Wittgenstein': A BBC Radio Talk by Elizabeth Anscombe in May 1953. *Nordic Wittgenstein Review* 8, 225–40

Floyd, J. (2016) Chains of Life: Turing, Lebensform, and the Emergence of Wittgenstein's Later Style. *Nordic Wittgenstein Review* 5:2, 7–89

Gabriel, G. (2018) Science and Fiction: A Fregean Approach. In G. Bengtsson, S. Säätelä, A. Pichler (eds.), *New Essays on Frege: Between Science and Literature*. Cham: Springer, 9–22

Glock, H.-J. (1996) *A Wittgenstein Dictionary*. Oxford: Wiley-Blackwell

Glock, H.-J. (2004) Was Wittgenstein an Analytic Philosopher? *Metaphilosophy* 35:4, 419–44

References

Glock, H.-J. (2024) Thinking in Style: Philosophy, Aesthetics and Writing in Wittgenstein's Work. In S. S. Grève (ed.), *Culture and Value after Wittgenstein*. Oxford: Oxford University Press.

Gorlée, D. L. (2020) *Wittgenstein's Secret Diaries: Semiotic Writing in Cryptography*. London: Bloomsbury Academic

Hacker, P. M. S. (2013) Wittgenstein's Anthropological and Ethnological Approach. In *Wittgenstein: Comparisons and Context*. Oxford: Oxford University Press, 111–27

Haller, R. (1988) *Questions on Wittgenstein*. London: Routledge

Hilmy, St. (1987) *The Later Wittgenstein*. Oxford: Blackwell

Immler, N. L. (2011) *Das Familiengedächtnis der Wittgensteins: Zu verführerischen Lesarten von (auto-)biographischen Texten*. Bielefeld: Transcript

Iven, M. (2015) Er ist eine Künstlernatur von hinreissender Genialität. Die Korrespondenz zwischen Ludwig Wittgenstein und Moritz Schlick sowie ausgewählte Briefe von und an Friedrich Waismann, Rudolf Carnap, Frank P. Ramsey, Ludwig Hänsel und Margaret Stonborough. *Wittgenstein-Studien* 6:1, 83–174

Janik, A. (1985) *Essays on Wittgenstein and Weininger*. Amsterdam: Rodopi

Janik, A. (2006) *Assembling Reminders: Studies in the Genesis of Wittgenstein's Concept of Philosophy*. Stockholm: Santerus

Janik, A. (2018) The Dichtung of Analytic Philosophy: Wittgenstein's Legacy from Frege and Its Consequences. In G. Bengtsson, S. Säätelä, A. Pichler (eds.), *New Essays on Frege: Between Science and Literature*. Cham: Springer, 143–57

Kahane, G., Kanterian, E., Kuusela, O. (2007) Introduction. In G. Kahane, E. Kanterian, O. Kuusela (eds.), *Wittgenstein and His Interpreters: Essays in Memory of Gordon Baker*. Oxford: Blackwell, 1–36

Kanterian, E. (2012) Philosophy as Poetry? Reflections on Wittgenstein's Style. *Wittgenstein-Studien* 3:1, 95–132

Keicher, P. (2000) Aspekte musikalischer Komposition bei Ludwig Wittgenstein: Studienfragmente zu D 302 und Opus MS 114ii/115i. In K. Neumer (ed.), *Das Verstehen des Anderen*. Frankfurt a.M.: Peter Lang, 199–255

Keicher, P. (2004) 'Ich wollte, alle diese Bemerkungen wären besser als sie sind'. – Vorworte und Vorwortentwürfe in Wittgensteins Nachlaß. In T. Demeter (ed.), *Essays on Wittgenstein and Austrian Philosophy: In Honour of J. C. Nyíri*. Amsterdam: Rodopi, 275–309

References

Kienzler, W., Sunday Grève, S. (2016) Wittgenstein on Gödelian 'Incompleteness', Proofs and Mathematical Practice: Reading Remarks on the Foundations of Mathematics, Part I, Appendix III, Carefully. In S. Sunday Grève, J. Mácha (eds.), *Wittgenstein and the Creativity of Language*. Basingstoke: Palgrave Macmillan, 76–116

Klagge, J. C. (2021) *Wittgenstein's Artillery: Philosophy as Poetry*. Cambridge: MIT Press

Krüger, H. W. (1993) Die Entstehung des *Big Typescript*. In J. Czermak, K. Puhl (eds.), *Wittgensteins Philosophie der Mathematik: Akten des 15. IWS, Teil 2*. Wien: Hölder-Pichler-Tempsky, 303–12

Leach, St. (2020) Chadbourne Gilpatric and Ludwig Wittgenstein: A Fateful Meeting. *Nordic Wittgenstein Review* 9, 209–29

Long, Chr. (2020) *Essays on Adolf Loos*. Prague: Kant

Maury, A. (1994) Sources of the remarks in Wittgenstein's *Philosophical Investigations*. *Synthese* 98, 349–78

Manninen, J. (2011) Waismann's Testimony of Wittgenstein's Fresh Starts 1931–35. In B. F. McGuinness (ed.), *Friedrich Waismann – Causality and Logical Positivism*. Dordrecht: Springer, 243–65

Mazzeo, M. (2021) *Logica e tumulti*. Macerata: Quodlibet

McGuinness, B. (1988) *Wittgenstein: A Life: Young Wittgenstein 1889–1921*. London: Duckworth

McGuinness, B. (2002a) Wittgenstein's 1916 'Abhandlung'. In Rudolf Haller, Klaus Puhl (eds.), *Wittgenstein and the Future of Philosophy: A Reassessment after 50 Years*. Vienna: Hölder-Pichler-Tempsky, 272–82

McGuinness, B. (2002b) *Approaches to Wittgenstein: Collected Papers*. London: Routledge

McGuinness, B. (2006a) Wittgenstein: Philosophy and literature. In A. Pichler, S. Säätelä (eds.), *Wittgenstein: The Philosopher and His Works*. Heusenstamm: ontos, 367–81

McGuinness, B. (2006b) In Praise of Nonsense. In R. Calcaterra (ed.), *Le ragioni del conoscere e dell'agire: Scritti in onore di Rosaria Egidi*. Milan: Franco Angeli, 357–65

McGuinness, B. (2010) Wittgenstein and Literature. In V. Munz, K. Puhl and J. Wang (eds.), *Language and World, Part 2: Signs, Minds and Actions*. Heusenstamm: ontos, 257–75

Misak, C. (2016) *Cambridge Pragmatism: From Peirce and James to Ramsey and Wittgenstein*. Oxford: Oxford University Press

Monk, R. (1990) *Ludwig Wittgenstein: The Duty of Genius*. London: Jonathan Cape.

Moyal-Sharrock, D. (2013) Beyond Hacker's Wittgenstein. *Philosophical Investigations* 36:4, 355–80

Munz, V. (2016) Philosophy from an 'Anthropological' Point of View: Wittgenstein and Sraffa. *Conceptus* 42:101–2, 66–82

Neumer, K. (2000) *Die Relativität der Grenzen: Studien zur Philosophie Wittgensteins*. Amsterdam: Rodopi

Nyíri, J. C. (1976) Wittgenstein's New Traditionalism. In J. Hintikka (ed.), *Essays on Wittgenstein in Honour of G. H. von Wright. Acta Philosophica Fennica* 28:1–3, 503–12

Nyíri, J. C. (1992) *Tradition and Individuality: Essays*. Dordrecht: Kluwer

Nyíri, J.C. (2006) Wittgenstein's Philosophy of Pictures. In A. Pichler, S. Säätelä (eds.), *Wittgenstein: The Philosopher and His Works*. Heusenstamm: ontos, 322–53

Ortner, H. (2000) *Schreiben und Denken*. Tübingen: Niemeyer

Perloff, M. (2004) Wittgenstein and the Question of Poetic Translatability. In J. Gibson, W. Huemer (eds.), *The Literary Wittgenstein*. London: Routledge, 34–54

Perloff, M. (2011) Writing Philosophy as Poetry: Literary form in Wittgenstein. In O. Kuusela, M. McGinn (eds.), *The Oxford Handbook of Wittgenstein*. Oxford: Oxford University Press, 714–28

Pichler, A. (2004) *Wittgensteins Philosophische Untersuchungen: Vom Buch zum Album*. Amsterdam: Rodopi

Pichler, A. (2006) 'Ich habe 14 Tage lang nichts gearbeitet ... ': Ein Blick auf die Schreibarbeit Wittgensteins. In J. Holzner, E. Sauermann (eds.), *Festschrift für Allan Janik. Mitteilungen aus dem Brenner-Archiv* 24–5. Innsbruck: Brenner-Forum, 131–49

Pichler, A. (2007) The Interpretation of the Philosophical Investigations: Style, Therapy, Nachlass. In G. Kahane, E. Kanterian, O. Kuusela (eds.), *Wittgenstein and His Interpreters: Essays in Memory of Gordon Baker*. Oxford: Blackwell, 123–44

Pichler, A. (2009) Wittgenstein's Albums: 'Philosophical Investigations' and 'Philosophical Remarks' as alternatives to the 'spirit of progress' in philosophy. In A. R. Moreno (ed.), *Wittgenstein – Como ler o álbum? Colecao CLE* 55, 57–97

Pichler, A. (2013a) Reflections on a Prominent Argument in the Wittgenstein Debate. *Philosophy and Literature* 37:2, 435–50

Pichler, A. (2013b) The Philosophical Investigations and Syncretistic Writing. In N. Venturinha (ed.), *The Textual Genesis of Wittgenstein's Philosophical Investigations*. New York: Routledge, 65–80

Pichler, A. (2016) Ludwig Wittgenstein and Us 'Typical Western Scientists'. In S. Sunday Grève, J. Mácha (eds.), *Wittgenstein and the Creativity of Language*. Basingstoke: Palgrave Macmillan, 55–75

Pichler, A. (2018) Wittgenstein on Understanding: Language, Calculus and Practice. In D. Stern (ed.), *Wittgenstein in the 1930s: Between the Tractatus and the Investigations*. Cambridge: Cambridge University Press, 45–60

Pichler, A. (2020) A Typology of the Philosopher Ludwig Wittgenstein's Writing of Text Alternatives. *Aisthesis. Pratiche, linguaggi e saperi dell'estetico* 13:2, 109–18

Pichler, A. (2023) What is a work by Wittgenstein? *Paradigmi* XLI 1, 129–46

Pilch, M. (2015) A Missing Folio at the Beginning of Wittgenstein's MS 104. *Nordic Wittgenstein Review* 4:2, 65–97

Pilch, M. (2022) Prototractatus. In A. Weiberg, St. Majetschak (eds.), *Wittgenstein Handbuch*. Berlin: Metzler, 58–61

Rhees, R. (1970) *Discussions of Wittgenstein*. London: Routledge and Kegan Paul

Rothhaupt, J. (2009) Wittgensteins 'philosophisches Akupunktieren' mit 'Bemerkungen'. In J. Bremer (ed.), *Ludwig Wittgenstein: 'Krakau zugeteilt' / 'przydzielony do Krakowa'*. Krakow: Ignatianum, 243–93

Rothhaupt, J. (2010) Wittgenstein at Work: Creation, Selection and Composition of 'Remarks'. In N. Venturinha (ed.), *Wittgenstein after His Nachlass*. Basingstoke: Palgrave Macmillan, 51–63

Rothhaupt, J. (2011) Der Komplex 'MS140(I)+MS114(II)+MS115(I)' als Wittgensteins Buch 'Lsrpmhmlsrhxsv Yvoviqfntvn'. In Ch. Jäger, W. Löffler (eds.), *Epistemology: Contexts, Values, Disagreement: Papers of the 34th IWS*. Kirchberg am Wechsel: ÖLWG, 247–50

Rothhaupt, J. (2015) Zur Genese der 'Philosophischen Untersuchungen' im engeren und im weiteren Sinne. In D. Moyal-Sharrock, V. Munz, A. Coliva (eds.), *Mind, Language and Action. Proceedings of the 36th IWS*. Berlin: De Gruyter, 205–54

Savickey, B. (2017) *Wittgenstein's Investigations*. Cham: Springer

Schalkwyk, D. (2004) Wittgenstein's 'Imperfect Garden': The Ladders and Labyrinths of Philosophy as *Dichtung*. In J. Gibson, W. Huemer (eds.), *The Literary Wittgenstein*. London: Routledge, 55–74

Schulte, J. (1990) *Chor und Gesetz: Wittgenstein im Kontext*. Frankfurt a. M.: Suhrkamp

Schulte, J. (1992) *Wittgenstein: An Introduction*. W. H. Brenner, J. F. Holley (trans.). Albany: SUNY Press

Schulte, J. (2006) What Is a Work by Wittgenstein? In A. Pichler, S. Säätelä (eds.), *Wittgenstein: The Philosopher and His Works*. Heusenstamm: ontos, 397–404

Somavilla, I. (2015) The Dimension of Silence in the Philosophy of Wittgenstein. In P. Hanna (ed.), *An Anthology of Philosophical Studies* vol. 9. Athens: Athens Institute for Education and Research, 121–32

Somavilla, I. (2020) Wittgenstein's Torments of the Mind. In S. Wuppuluri, N. da Costa (eds.), *Wittgensteinian: Looking at the World from the Viewpoint of Wittgenstein's Philosophy*. Cham: Springer, 535–57

Stern, D. G. (1995) *Wittgenstein on Mind and Language*. Oxford: Oxford University Press

Stern, D. G. (1996) The Availability of Wittgenstein's Philosophy. In D. G. Stern, H. Sluga (eds.), *The Cambridge Companion to Wittgenstein*. Cambridge: Cambridge University Press, 442–76

Stern, D. G. (2004) *Wittgenstein's Philosophical Investigations: An Introduction*. Cambridge: Cambridge University Press

Stern, D. G. (2016) The University of Iowa Tractatus Map. *Nordic Wittgenstein Review* 5:2, 203–20

Stern, D. G. (2017) Wittgenstein's Texts and Style. In H.-J. Glock, J. Hyman (eds.), *A Companion to Wittgenstein*. Oxford: Wiley-Blackwell, 41–55

Sunday Grève, S. (2015) The Importance of Understanding Each Other in Philosophy. *Philosophy* 90:2, 213–39

Trächtler, J. (2021) *Wittgensteins Grammatik des Fremdseelischen*. Stuttgart: Metzler

Uffelmann, S. A. (2018) *Vom System zum Gebrauch: Eine genetisch-philosophische Untersuchung des Grammatikbegriffs bei Wittgenstein*. Berlin: De Gruyter

Venturinha, N. (2013) Introduction. In N. Venturinha (ed.), *The Textual Genesis of Wittgenstein's Philosophical Investigations*. New York: Routledge, 1–16

Venturinha, N. (2018) Agrammaticality. In G. Bengtsson, S. Säätelä, A. Pichler (eds.), *New Essays on Frege: Between Science and Literature*. Cham: Springer, 159–75

Wallgren, T. (2006) *Transformative Philosophy: Socrates, Wittgenstein, and the Democratic Spirit of Philosophy*. Maryland: Lexington Books

Wallgren, Th. (ed.) (2023) *The Creation of Wittgenstein*. London: Bloomsbury

Westergaard, P. K. (1995) A Note on Wittgenstein and Loos. In K. S. Johannessen, T. Nordenstam (eds.), *Culture and Value – Philosophy and the Cultural Sciences: Papers of the 18th IWS*. Kirchberg am Wechsel: ÖLWG, 284–91

Wright, G. H. von (1969) Special Supplement: The Wittgenstein Papers. *Philosophical Review* 78:4, 483–503

Wright, G. H. von (1982) *Wittgenstein*. Oxford: Blackwell

Wright, G. H. von (1992) The Troubled History of Part II of the 'Investigations'. *Grazer Philosophische Studien* 42:1, 181–92

Wright, G. H. von (1993) *The Tree of Knowledge and Other Essays*. Leiden: Brill

Zambito, P. F. (forthcoming) Essayism as a Form of Writing and a Form of Life. *Orbis Litterarum*. https://onlinelibrary.wiley.com/doi/full/10.1111/oli.12317

Acknowledgements

Throughout the years, I could discuss ideas that have become part of this Element with countless colleagues and friends and I am much obliged to all of them. For detailed discussion of parts of the Element I am deeply grateful to Nivedita Gangopadhyay, Ralph Jewell and Thomas Wallgren. I would also like to thank two anonymous reviewers and series editor David G. Stern for their valuable suggestions and comments.

Cambridge Elements

The Philosophy of Ludwig Wittgenstein

David G. Stern
University of Iowa

David G. Stern is a Professor of Philosophy and a Collegiate Fellow in the College of Liberal Arts and Sciences at the University of Iowa. His research interests include history of analytic philosophy, philosophy of language, philosophy of mind, and philosophy of science. He is the author of *Wittgenstein's Philosophical Investigations: An Introduction* (Cambridge University Press, 2004) and *Wittgenstein on Mind and Language* (Oxford University Press, 1995), as well as more than 50 journal articles and book chapters. He is the editor of *Wittgenstein in the 1930s: Between the 'Tractatus' and the 'Investigations'* (Cambridge University Press, 2018) and is also a co-editor of the *Cambridge Companion to Wittgenstein* (Cambridge University Press, 2nd edition, 2018), *Wittgenstein: Lectures, Cambridge 1930–1933, from the Notes of G. E. Moore* (Cambridge University Press, 2016) and *Wittgenstein Reads Weininger* (Cambridge University Press, 2004).

About the Series
This series provides concise and structured introductions to all the central topics in the philosophy of Ludwig Wittgenstein. The Elements are written by distinguished senior scholars and bright junior scholars with relevant expertise, producing balanced and comprehensive coverage of the full range of Wittgenstein's thought.

Cambridge Elements

The Philosophy of Ludwig Wittgenstein

Elements in the Series

Wittgenstein's Heirs and Editors
Christian Erbacher

Wittgenstein on Aspect Perception
Avner Baz

Reading Wittgenstein's Tractatus
Mauro Luiz Engelmann

Wittgenstein on Sense and Grammar
Silver Bronzo

Wittgenstein on Logic and Philosophical Method
Oskari Kuusela

Wittgenstein on Sense and Grammar
Silver Bronzo

Wittgenstein on Forms of Life
Anna Boncompagni

Wittgenstein on Criteria and Practices
Lars Hertzberg

Wittgenstein on Religious Belief
Genia Schönbaumsfeld

Wittgenstein and Aesthetics
Hanne Appelqvist

Style, Method and Philosophy in Wittgenstein
Alois Pichler

A full series listing is available at: www.cambridge.org/EPLW

Printed in the United States
by Baker & Taylor Publisher Services